WE ESCAPED
TO THE
COUNTRY

AND IT RAINED
CATS & DOGS – AND DONKEYS

BARBARA FLEMING

ALSO BY BARBARA FLEMING

Lewes, Two thousand Years of History (now out of print)

The Battle of Lewes 1264 (now out of print)

The Discontented Waterpots (a play) (now out of print)

The Fishermen of Jesus

Three Men in a Book: Heroes of the Bible

Your Path to the Kingdom

Hooray! We Have Found the Holy Spirit!

Hooray! We Have Found the Kingdom!

Hooray! We Have Found Our Hero

WE ESCAPED
TO THE
COUNTRY

AND IT RAINED
CATS & DOGS – AND DONKEYS

MEMOIRS
Cirencester

Published by Memoirs

MEMOIRS
PUBLISHING

25 Market Place, Cirencester, Gloucestershire, GL7 2NX
info@memoirsbooks.co.uk www.memoirspublishing.com

ISBN: 978-1-909544-98-7

WE ESCAPED
TO THE
COUNTRY

This Book is dedicated to: -
Conker, Lucy, Toffee, Poppy, Tinker
and Merlin and all those who gave us
so much joy and love.

TABLE OF CONTENTS

CHAPTER I

THE GREAT ESCAPE

There was this man Noah, with all the threatening waters of the World gathering against him, who jumped onto his boat, piled in all his family and pets and cast off for a better life beyond the flood. That just shows how history repeats itself. A few thousand years later here we were, Noahs of the 20th century, being flooded out by the grasping tide of materialism which threatened to drown all the things we valued most, two grown-ups, three young offspring, one pet cat and one small, pet mouse, all casting around for a life-line to safety.

Our ship of rescue turned out to be one very basic, sit-up-and-beg, Ford Anglia, purchased for one hundred and seventy pounds from a friend of a friend. And our compass pointed South.

The Mr. Noah in our family wasn't a boat-builder, or a car builder, though come to think of it he did work for Shell Tankers. He commuted daily by London train to the Minories. His wife and hand-maid, myself, cooked, cleaned, shopped and pottered in the time-honoured fashion of mothers in the Sixties, and produced the three girl offspring to measure up to the three sons of the Old Testament. .

There was Katherine, a bit of us both, but the biggest share entirely her own invention. There was Elizabeth, who was the source of all the menagerie we had collected so far, one tortoiseshell tabby kitten, called Tinker, one white mouse and a stick-insect. Not just one stick insect, actually, when we discovered that the 'funny black bits at the bottom of the jar' were really eggs. After that we successfully hatched hundreds of baby stick-insects in the airing-cupboard!

Lastly there was young Jenny, not yet six, but already absorbing all these animal requirements of Elizabeth and tucking them away for future reference and innocently enquiring at regular intervals, "Oh Please, when are we going to get a dog?"

One pet cat and one small mouse

In all it had felt very cosy, safe and enduring within our suburban corner of Greater London that seemed so comfortable and so complete, when it suddenly started to rain! The first drops, I can vividly remember, were in the shape of (funny to think of it now) Walkie-talkie dolls for little girls' birthday presents, and frightfully expensive, king-size watches for small boys. And then, fantastic, swimming pools in people's back-gardens and two cars in every drive! Then wireless metamorphosed into television sets and the pound began its long climb up to its lofty throne of the present day.

Before we knew it, we were being scooped up into a new age of money and make-believe, of plausibility and plastic. The century had turned, the lingering shadow of war had gone at last, the Sixties was flying the delusion of a Brave New World before our eyes, an age of finance, oil, power - and wheels..

But, as I said, it was the wheels that rescued us from the Flood. Cars! They crowded off the factory belts, bubbles of colour down a stream that flowed unending into the highways and byways of the land. Suddenly everybody found they needed one and off they floated, out of their tiny, fenced-in lives in city, town and suburb, into the wide, wide world of field and furrow, shady wood and   Downs. Wild life fled from the clank of hedgers, ditchers and the throb of combines. Man soared into the sky, blasting white vapour trails where once the larks had sung. And in the country lanes, suddenly the hoot and snort of cars unravelled a thousand tangled ways and shouted to the World, "Come on! Leave all the hurly burly of the towns, the countryside is yours. Yours to explore, yours to enjoy, yours for the taking!"

Suddenly we too had a car like everyone else! A spartan, heater-less wagon, but nonetheless a car and, just as suddenly, I found myself floating off - well, sitting behind the wheel actually-persuaded that my ambition was to find a safe, secure anchorage for myself, my family, and perhaps even a dog, and of course the stick-insects, as far away from the whirlpool of moneymaking, of materialism, of aggrandisement and petty competitiveness as I could. I set off. The little car bounced happily along the country lanes. The Spring was pleasant and the hedges were busy decorating their feet with primroses. I dived headlong, five hundred feet down the chalk escarpment and came to the first village in the Weald...

... Six months later, when Autumn was thinking about folding all her rainbow coloured dresses away for the winter, I was still bouncing and a lot further afield.

I expect it was partly my fault and not entirely that of the house-agents. What with all this talk of country houses and dogs, they must have become completely confused and sent me to houses that looked awfully like dog kennels quite by mistake. .

When I waxed especially eloquent, somewhere around East Grinstead, I found myself solemnly viewing four posts and half a roof, in the middle of nowhere, that would have proved rather draughty for a dog but actually did house half-a-dozen chickens!

I soberly retraced my steps up the half-mile of stony stream that doubled as a front drive to the chicken house and sat back in my car.... perhaps a man's voice, from my side of the counter, could explain it all more clearly.

Anyway, it was obvious that I needed moral, if not physical, support and as Keith's gardening-fork and cricket-bat were in hibernation now, until next summer, it seemed an ideal time to enlist the family in my search.

So now, altogether, at weekends, we explored a succession of musty kitchens and echoing Victorian villas. There were cottages that huddled under huge, threatening hedges, and houses, nearly all with crumbling floor-boards, with railway embankments that towered above their chimney pots.

There were hovels that shivered along terrifying main roads and shacks that looked sadly at us from the depths of mournful, rain-soaked woods. We went west... we went south... as far south as I dared suggest since every mile meant, up at the crack of dawn for Keith and a railway season-ticket the size of the National Debt!

Christmas came and went. The children retired, gracefully from the fray. Their overall ambition to move house had not lost its ardour, but their keenness on driving a hundred miles in a freezing car, every Saturday, had. I had not the heart to blame them when, "No thank you," they said politely. "We think we'll stay and look after Tinker the cat this weekend." "We'll be fine, really," and added sweetly, "Have a nice time." It was a momentous day though, they shouldn't have missed it.

We drove off, Keith and I. The sky was ominous above and the ice crackled below. To hearten us even further we passed a mangled motor-bike and car by the roadside. Our wheels crunched doggedly on as we headed south and the wintry Weald froze steadily around us.

Lewes Town

I felt like Hudson trying to find the North West Passage and perhaps, like him, we were going to be imprisoned in some desolate spot, held fast by. pack-ice, and dug out frozen and stiff months afterwards by a sad-faced search-party.

"What was the first address then?" Keith's highly practical voice demolished my nightmares. We drew up in front of quite the most hideous house I had seen to date. The main road hurtled past its front gate and a wall of giant elms defended it from any vestige of light or sun. We drove on in silence to the next on the list... and the next...

The light was going altogether as I folded all the maps away dejectedly. I looked sideways at Keith. His face was impassive as he stared out at the first drifting snowflakes.

"We'll go home a different way," he said. "It will be sheltered under the Downs. I'll make for Ditchling."

The Gods of that part of Sussex looked down on us from their groves on the heights. I don't know to this day if they really demeaned themselves so much as to take pity on us. Perhaps we had just worn them down at last, as we had worn down their House-agents, their roads and our tyres!

Anyway they suddenly decided that they would, at long last, actually consider accepting us. Graciously they agreed that they would allow us just one glimpse of that very small corner that should, for us from now on, be 'forever Sussex'.

We were almost beyond feeling as they led us through the blinding snowstorm along the foot of the Downs, into their favourite town already shuttered and half-asleep in the growing dark.

We pulled up at the railway station. "LEWES" it proclaimed itself.

"Lets just see what a Season-ticket costs from here," grunted Keith, mesmerised probably by the cold.

He climbed stiffly out and disappeared through the uninviting doorway.

A minute or two later he climbed thoughtfully back in again and sat frowning at the wheel in puzzled silence.

"You go in," he said eventually. "I must have heard it wrong." I wonder what the station-attendant thought at being asked the same out of the way question twice, in a quick, three minutes? He patiently returned the same, unbelievable answer and we found that we had made the great discovery that, in those days anyway, the further you travelled on your daily journey, the cheaper, per mile, became your season-ticket. It seemed a fairy tale come true.

By this time I, for one, was falling over myself with eagerness to believe anything, fairy tales, the lot, that would lead us to just one, cheap, rambling house in one, cheap, rambling acre of English countryside.

We wandered up the deserted High Street. No harm in just looking in the agents windows... and there, in the very first one, complete with a picture, with five bedrooms and an acre of countryside, was exactly the house we had sought so long for our family... and for our hypothetical dog!

CHAPTER II

DIGGING IN

Now if you are not interested in houses, but only in animals, you can skip the next, few pages, for they are going to be mostly about the house. You see, without the house, the story would never have gone further than here and perhaps we should, even now, be still existing, stranded and dog less for ever, on our suburban shores.

Besides which, the house would have been extremely hurt. He has his feelings like the rest of us and, when you get to the ripe, old age of a hundred and two, you need to be respected and pampered a little.

He had a good laugh when I drove up to the gate, the following week, all starry-eyed. The first thing that hit me was this simply enormous pine-tree that looked as though he owned the place and the second thing was the railway line that he had been hiding behind his back. Suitably subdued, I ploughed my way through the brambles to the front door.

They never did get it open! They tugged and I pushed. I shoved and they heaved. But it never moved an inch. In the end we all gave it up and transferred ourselves round to the back of the house and then I crossed the threshold at last.

It was not too impressive inside, I had to admit. In fact the first surveyor's report, politely translated, read; "Personally, I would not be found stone dead in the place!" I could see his point. He probably came from an elegant, brick edifice in the middle of Hove or Brighton and, anyway, he didn't have three determined children and an equally determined, imaginary dog snapping at his heels.

The house thought it was a huge joke.

"They haven't seen anything yet, have they, Pine-tree?" he chuckled.

"Just wait till they get to know of the damp in the Study floor! And how about my poor old cracked drains, the blocked soakaways, the broken sash-cords and woodworm everywhere?" But he had reckoned without Keith, for one.

Keith comes from a long line of ancient and skilled coalminers. He was born and bred within sight of heaven knows how many coal-pits in county Durham and he has inherited all the 'delving' instincts of Wycliff's original Adam.

His very favourite occupation of all is nosing down into blocked drains. He loves digging big holes and his next-to-favourite occupation is taking up floor-boards.

Dog-kennel extraordinary

He once nearly netted a CID man down his best hole of all! He had dug it in the middle of our drive in Sanderstead on the darkest night of the winter, when it was pouring with rain. The CID man just happened to be dropping in about some local burglaries and he very nearly did drop in, too. He was terribly impressed with it as a professional burglar-trap, but I hate to think what his opinion of it would have been if he hadn't caught sight of it, at his feet, just in time.

Yes, Keith and the old house got on famously from the first moment when, six months and endless negotiations later, we bumped down the brick-dust drive (in pouring rain) to take possession of our 'dog-kennel extraordinary' at last! That sounds almost like the end of the story, doesn't it? But it isn't! In fact the exciting part was only just beginning! And, fond though he has since turned out to be of as many dogs, cats, donkeys etc. as we have supplied him with, the house insisted that his needs must come first.

So, with a thousand pounds of our mortgage-loan held back until we had repaired him to the Building Society's (and his) satisfaction, we had to postpone turning him into any sort of a kennel for at least six busy months.

Dear old house! He won't admit it, even to his best friend the pine tree, but I believe he came to like us almost as much as we loved him. We washed his cracked, wrinkled face with two coats of white cement-paint and he looked years younger even before the summer was out. We re-cemented the drains and Keith bored all sorts of rabbit-warrens through the soak-aways to redirect the drainage. We threw out all the rotting kitchen cupboards, scraped the grease off the walls and then went to investigate the Study. That was the day that we lost Keith altogether. Well, Jenny was positive she had seen him going into the Study. But when we looked there was no sign. "Daddy!" we called frantically all through the house and the out-buildings.

"Keith!" my voice, slightly tinged now with vague, imaginings that he might have dug one hole too many and disappeared down it like Alice's rabbit. "Keith!..." And then a muffled echo reached us from right under our feet.

"I just thought I would get right down under here and have a good look round..!" and a cobweb-encrusted mop of black, curly hair bobbed up through an unbelievably tiny hole in the corner of the floor-boards.

For some days after that it became his, and Tinker's favourite recreation to 'have a good look down-under.'

After that, floor-boards came up in one room after another all through the house. The electricians vied with the wood-worm sprayers and Keith ran them a valiant third place. Tinker had the time of her life, especially in the attic bedrooms which had delicious mouse-nests under practically every other board. Yes, the house had its own particular brand of animal occupants even before we arrived.

It was very like a story out of a Beatrix Potter book the way the mice frisked in and out of the holes in the floors in nearly every room. When we arrived with all our goods and chattels that first day, complete with our own, enchanting, but ~ rather smelly (because he was a boy) mouse, it was probably as good an example, in all time, of the old adage "Carrying coals to Newcastle". In blissful ignorance however we arrived and deliberated long and carefully which of the various out-buildings would best suit the smallest member of our tribe.

The byres seemed a bit remote. We suspected that 'out of scent' would have soon been 'out of mind' and he might have ended up one very starved little mouse.

The garages were too cold and the coalshed too,

although it did have an awfully tempting shelf. Hard lines on the coal-man though and whoever filled the coal buckets every day!

He finally came to rest in the wash-house where his fruity smell was a continuous reminder to, "Close the door before the smell walks through!" He would have loved it up in the attic-rooms of course, but even in the washhouse I guess he woke up that night believing we had transferred him to Mouse-Paradise. I expect he had the time of his young life enthralling the 'natives' with yarns, as long as his tail, of the great Mouse Metropolis he had come from. It was "Town mouse, Country mouse" all over again and the local clans enjoyed it hugely.

Soon the wash-house was alive with white and brown mice and a very interesting mixture of both. We did try to be sympathetic. 'Live and let live', we thought. But I finally drew the line at a tail cheekily whisking its way out through the LARDER grating in the back-kitchen. Even then it was a long tussle and it took us all of seven years to gently (or otherwise) persuade the local mice inhabitants that they ought to keep to their side of the house, the OUT-side.

Our tame mouse was eventually replaced by a succession of hamsters and these graduated, by junior tact and guile, to all sorts of rooms around the house, ending up in the sitting-room where Hammy shared his nightly vigil with the cat. As they were both night-workers by habit it is anybody's guess how they passed away the hours of darkness. By the tell-tale deposits around the cage, sometimes I guess an over-bold field-mouse must have still ventured in to wine and dine with his exotic cousin.

But Tinker merely gave a sleepy yawn and stretched an innocent paw... When Hammy lived in the bathroom now, the goings-on weren't nearly so well controlled! Goodness knows what they all got up to until one night when I was engrossed in my usual bath-time reading, I could have sworn a small dark 'something' had suddenly disappeared into the hamster's cage. And before the end of my page I was plumb certain that it had, because it suddenly whisked back into the airing-cupboard to tell its Mum that supper was served.

Goaded into drastic action beyond my usual capabilities, I baited the cupboard with mouse-poison and hoped that the curtain would ring down (while I was well out of the way) on that extra mouse-diversion. Which it did - well, practically!

Then there came that bitter, winter morning when I shivered my way into the bathroom, only half-awake as usual, to find a tiny, furry object lying frozen stiff in the ice-cold bath. I remember how carefully I lifted him out and took him downstairs into the less arctic regions. I popped him down in the still-warm sitting-room grate and had to leave him, such a mournful little corpse, while we mustered for the daily chaos of breakfast-and-off-to-school.

When peace reigned again, I crept back into the sitting-room and watched with bated breath as suddenly one whisker flickered into life and then another.

When he had reached the 'beginning to crawl' stage it suddenly dawned on me that total recovery, where he was, might prove embarrassing to both of us. So I hastily transferred him back into the airing-cupboard plus, of course, a dish of nicely warmed milk and rich, wholemeal biscuits to restore him to health and strength! I'll never learn....

So much for the house and its inhabitants.

But we hadn't just taken possession of a house, we had planted ourselves onto an acre of solid Sussex clay as well... or thought we had.

The paddock had been kept in some sort of seemliness by half a dozen bullocks, the hedges were well cropped and the boundaries trampled to rock hardness underfoot.

The garden had run wild, however, for at least ten years. It snorted in derision at our town-size spade and our dainty lawn-mower.

"They can soften you up with their paint and plaster as much as they like" he jeered at the house in his warm Sussex accent, "But it'll take a lot more than them simpering ways to get me tamed."

The pine-tree loftily umpired as battle was joined, and. I've a pretty good idea whose side he was on by the ton and a half of pine-needles he deluged us with to start the fray.

All five of us in the family took turns in our individual ways to reduce the jungle- grass to garden-lawn. I tried to penetrate it with my faithful little hand-mower and was bounced out of the ring in no uncertain fashion.

Katherine and Jenny, who always liked doing the same things in the same way, emerged shyly holding a pair of scissors each and triumphantly trimmed almost a square foot of meadow before they announced, "It must be time for tea!"

Elizabeth, with touching concern, emerged from the house complete with her pet hamster who she thought 'might be able to eat quite a lot of it for us'. She said she had heard that guinea-pigs were very good at grass-cutting too and she knew where there were some going "Very cheap"...

Keith was the only one to really come to grips with the problem. After his masterful triumph over the drains and the damp there was no holding him. Off he drove and bought a real country-type grass-cutter that the man assured him would cut acres and acres of grass - which it did.

Actually, I reckon it bluffed its way through by puffing out thick clouds of black dragon-smoke and, short of a whistle, could almost be mistaken for the Flying Scot it made so much noise. Still, the garden suddenly found it was becoming less and less like Darkest Africa and more and more like a front lawn and it swiftly called its rearguard defences to march into action:

The rallying cry went out, "All moles in the land unite!"

The Old-Pine

And they sharpened their little spades and flocked in from far and near to carve out an underground system under our land to rival that of the London Tube.

Pyramids of soft, brown loam appeared like mushrooms overnight. They marched in soldier-like rows this way and that until the grass became one massed 'parade-ground' of mole-hills. If you were very sharp-eyed and a lot less clumsy than we usually were, you could even spot a little pink snout and tiny fat, waving fingers that with a "Look, no hands!" jibe, would turn in a twinkling of an eye and disappear out of sight like a neat conjuring trick.

One thing was crystal clear. We could either have a lawn or we could have moles. But it was humanly impossible to have both.

Looking around all the fields that lapped up to our hedges like green waves of the sea on every side, we felt there ought to be room for both of us in the world if we could only persuade the Mole Unions to see it our way.

George, from the village (Cooks bridge) who came in first to help with the vegetable-garden on the other side of the drive, was certain that his mole-traps would do the trick. They were rather rusty contraptions of museum vintage and he parked them artfully 'along them runs' at such curious intervals that all we caught in them was our toes and sometimes our fingers too for good measure, and the little moles heaved up another shoulderful of earth, all round they were shaking so much with laughter. We tried a modern type of molefuse. You lit the blue paper and retired immediately. The children found them almost as much fun as Fire-work Night. But the moles were Sussex bred and down here they have been experts in fireworks for more than three hundred years. They thrive on the smell of gun-powder. . .

I delved into endless gardening books for ideas.

On the instructions of one, we solemnly planted lines of moth-balls (which I had quite a job finding in the shops) across the land so that, to the average mole, our field and garden were as well-mined as Paschendale Ridge. Perhaps they were, and some did succumb. We never knew for, if they did, their losses were more than adequately re-inforced by the neighbouring moledivisions.

Eventually, but long enough afterwards for the moles

and the garden to have chalked it up as their battle well and truly won, we invested in a very long hose-pipe, one that stretched to the limits of our lawn. The moles conceded us a local victory in the face of determined flooding. But, generous to the last, they left us with their piles of soft, beautifully worked soil, the ideal potting-mixture for tiny plants trying to wriggle their delicate toes into the heavy, Wealden clay.

They popped back occasionally just to see if we really were still there. But by now our defences were more or less fool-proof. No thanks to the gardening books of the world either.

They retreated as silently as they had come, their dignity unimpaired, preferring the much more peaceful company of the cows beyond the railway-line to the inquisitive noses and determined pawings of our DOGS

CHAPTER III

PUPPIES ALL ROUND AND LUCKY PAUL!

Yes, at last our house was tidied and the garden tamed- well, half tamed- and that's as much as it ever would be, and we could offer a home, "Fit for a dog to live in".

But where did one find a dog, in the country, I wondered?

We were out of the orbit of our sawdust-smelling Arcade in Croydon and not yet one enough with the countryside to be in the know of, "Mrs. Thatched-cottage, over the hill, who wants a home for her litter of lovely puppies".

I cast about swiftly, with one ear cocked for the ominous approach of Elizabeth trailing a little caravan of mouth-watering waifs and strays. They would surely have been great bargain offers but...

It was time to act and to act fast! I tracked down a Rescue Centre, eventually, It was a nice, friendly place and simply full of dogs all shapes and sizes and all needing homes. On my second visit, I had the sense to

22

take along our level-headed Katherine. For such a naive Mum, I am so lucky to have picked such a logically-minded daughter at first attempt. We started at the puppy run and worked our way steadily (and firmly) round the enclosure. The clamorous barking of over twenty dogs followed our slow procession. It was heart-rending. It was also deafening!

Eventually, to my relief, I found myself safely shepherded back to the start again without having acquired any enormous Alsatians or even that rather disapproving looking Boxer. Katherine stopped in front of the puppies again and I stopped too. Behind us coaxing, bullying, shouting dogs were all barking at once, "I'm the one you want."

"Take me. Take me."

But in the corner of the kindergarten cage there was one small brown imp who had curled himself up in complete unconcern for anybody in the world's likes or dislikes.

If we took him out or not, it was all one to him, he had gone fast to sleep! We took him.

Unrolled, he turned out to be mostly black with bits of brown. He was smooth-haired with small flopped-over ears and great fun. So small too. I had particularly wanted one that would only grow to about twelve inches and one that would be a nice sturdy mongrel with no perplexing pedigree weaknesses.

We tried out a string of original names on him but when Autumn came and his very favourite game turned out to be the thorough redistribution of the five thousand chestnuts that littered the ground at the front gate, we called him 'Conker'.

He was all he had promised to be.. nice, sturdy and a mongrel. When it came to growing it was a different matter.

When he reached the required twelve inches he found he couldn't quite explore the draining board as well as he would like to, so he grew another couple of inches.

But in doing so, he was able to get his first glimpse of the sink-basket. He grew the needed extra two inches or so to sample its contents.

There wasn't much we could do about it, except keep the sink-basket constantly cleared. Like Topsy he 'just grew'. He put the brake on somewhere just under Alsatian dimensions He could reach all he wanted by then!

And that was our very first dog.

I am sure, being such green-horns, we weren't the best owners in the world by a long way, but we did love him very much. We wanted everybody else to love him too.

With true converts' enthusiasm we even went another step forward and wanted everybody else to have a dog of their own to love too. . ..

My oldest friend, Bar, little knew what a noose she was running her head into when she came to spend the day with us. Conker had just come back from a long and exciting rabbit-chase (I never did manage to stop him), whenever I called frantically after him he used to turn considerately and give me a charming, airy wave and disappear through the nearest hedge.

So he was full and tired and very pleased with himself as he stretched himself elegantly out over the hearthrug at our feet and looked every inch a gentleman.

Bar was quite taken in. She mildly ventured that her growing Paul could do with a puppy himself.

When I think back on what followed, it speaks volumes for her good nature and our long-standing friendship that we are still even on speaking terms.

"Why of course," I pounced. "Up on the hill there are the loveliest puppies imaginable."

"No, they never run away. Their mother dog just sits happily at the end of her driveway and watches the world go by in the nicest possible way."

"No, they never fight. So cuddly and tiny too." "Just the kind you need in your town house and awfully cheap..."

Like a couple of innocents we hastened to our doom and from the pile of plump, wriggling puppies we picked the plumpest and the wriggliest - Jack Russell terrier.

Goodness, we have come a long way in the dog-world since that day. And what we didn't know then (and have learned the hard way since) is that a Jack Russell dog, especially the smooth-haired variety which this was, is a very special kind of terrier. It looks the picture of innocence and just the most manageable dog that was ever invented. In reality, it is bred for two things only. The first is hunting. The second is killing!

Lucky Paul

They are bred small not, surprisingly, to make them more cuddly, or even so that you can pop them more easily into your shopping basket. Or even to take up less room beside you and your hot-water bottle in bed. They are bred small so that they can tunnel down badger-setts and fox-earth's where those needle-like fangs deal out death, fierce and bloody, to anything they meet.

What is more, they have little jaws that are so strong that, when   they are locked into the neck of another dog as they frequently are, it can take two strong men to pull them apart and then to keep them apart afterwards. They are killers because they are bred for killing. They adore fighting and often roam far and wide to track down a hopeful quarry and if that sounds the ideal pet for anybody's cherished infant to cut his teeth on, they must be some teeth!

Bar's young son was, luckily, of a fairly tough breed himself and the puppy started off as very tiny...

The children were terribly envious,

"Oh, lucky Paul, When can we see the puppy?"

And (out of earshot of Conker I am glad to say) a wistful,

"Couldn't we have one too?"

"Well," I temporised, "They are bound to be going on holiday in the summer. I expect we could look after him for them then."

Yes, that was a good idea. How Conker would love having a playmate all for himself and what fun it would be for everybody. It was, actually, but not quite the way we had planned.

Conker made his visitor nicely welcome, showed him the smelliest corners with pride and then took him for a lovely long walk, just the two of them together.

I was mildly surprised when the local game-keeper arrived at the door with our squirming little visitor in his arms.

"Better keep him in," he said darkly "Might come to some harm with all those pheasants about."

Don't tell anyone, but in my inexperience I actually took it to mean that Paddy might be set on by the pheasants!

And then our life exploded.

Conker's minute playmate suddenly took a flying leap into the air and hung on in an altogether unexpected, but extremely business-like way, to the thick ruff of fur around his neck. Bright red blood spurted out in all directions at once. It showed up in glorious technicolour on the snow-white fur of the puppy. It looked nearly as effective on the white bits of our hall wall-paper.

It was all rather shattering but very educational.

The unwarranted attacks continued, on and off for the whole three weeks of Paddy's holiday. I can't think how Tinker managed to stay alive through it all as well as us. Conker was made mostly of bone and muscle so he was the best equipped of all to cope. He recognised that he had a lot to learn though. Paddy was happy to continue his tuition.

He showed him how to leap gaily up the forbidden stair-case onto the landing and to flood the new bedroom carpets with pools of indelible yellow liquid. To this day they mark the occasion by puzzling patches of green in an otherwise blue expanse.

Even the wall-paper above the skirting-boards came in for their full share of the deluge, Conker scrupulously copying his infant teacher in careful procession. We quickly got adjusted to it all. The house has never looked the same spruce old gentleman he originally was in his lovely new wall-paper, but we almost came to enjoy the excitement really.

The one commendable characteristic of a Jack Russell became immediately obvious, at least it is small enough and light enough to be instantly transportable from the scene of the fights once you had managed the dis-entangling part. Moreover, attending with concentration his crash- course on dog-handling as we did, we learned a terrific lot on the subject in those three eventful weeks.

So much so, that when the time came to return him to his owner the house seemed quite empty and almost dull. "It would be nice for Conk to have a brother, wouldn't it?" mused Elizabeth.

"He might like a sister as well," put in Jenny. "Two dogs are lovely company for each other.. or even three..."

I could see the familiar siege equipment being wheeled into position. "Dogs cost money to keep, you know," I reminded all of us firmly. "And we still have not saved enough to finish all the re-wiring."

The children wisely crept away. They had sown the seed, now they would wait for it to germinate. The house was on their side too, I knew that well enough. He adored company. He loved his old doors being banged by lots of children and his windows rattling in their frames to the shouts of happy laughter. What he would have loved most would have been for us to throw wide the doors and invite hundreds of people, two-legged or four, he wasn't fussy, to come in and make themselves at home in him for ever and ever.

All very well for him. He didn't have to make their beds and do the washing up... Still, I did have to admit, we did have room for more pets even if we did not have the bank-balance to sustain them. While I keep

Bar and the infamous Paddy

you in suspense for the spine-chilling solution, let me finish the Awful Tale of Paddy the Pup for you. He had a riotous career and it is too good not to be told.

He spent seven or eight highly irrepressible years being the Holy Terror of his neighbourhood.

He barked threats like a continuous rattle of machine-gun fire whenever he was let free into the backgarden. His greatest joy (and skill) was to hurtle out of the front-door and disappear in a cloud of dust and war-cries into the limitless suburban battle-ground beyond.

He plunged into fights on sight. He was almost run over incessantly. He wandered for miles and was for ever being returned by exhausted and reproachful rescuers. He was a coil of charged energy every waking moment (and there were a great many of those). When he was 'at home' he would tear round the furniture like a mad thing whenever the door-bell rang. When kennelled locally, he barked his voice to a hoarse standstill in one ear-splitting week.

Bar endured it all.

She even taught him to sit (for about a minute at a time), to be clean and to be quiet at night. His wickedly intelligent brown eyes could be meltingly endearing when it suited him. As a lost and lonely stray he could act the part of deserted waif with convincing artistry.

Bar gave up even bothering to report his 'desertions' to the police station. The phone would invariably ring eventually and a kindly voice would gently reassure her that her dear little doggy was quite safe and was tucked up in a nice warm kitchen/sitting-room/bedroom, waiting to be given a free lift back to his 'distraught' owner.

At last, when the family went their separate ways, she had to find a new home for him altogether.

She advertised him tentatively and truthfully (well, as near as one dared) in the local paper. Within hours of the paper being on the streets her phone was ringing with a queue of would-be Paddy-owners that never stopped.

After the eleventh caller she turned the rest away.

The next day the chosen, elderly couple arrived to adopt him. He hurled himself at, around, over and under them in his worst behaviour possible.

They adored it!

He barked uproariously until they were deafened. They were frankly delighted.

Then he performed his one and only party-trick of trotting over and shutting the door with such incorrigible impudence that they were enslaved for ever.

They marched off into their eventful new life together as happy as three children going for a picnic. What is more, they even rang back the next day to say how very grateful they both were and how marvellously they were all getting on together - and, knowing dogs, I expect they still are!

CHAPTER IV

GOING TO THE DOGS

To be perfectly honest, I cannot say that Conker spent any noticeable hours moping over the departure of his first playmate. He was a loner at heart.

He probably said to himself, like I did, after another car- load of visitors had disappeared up the drive.

"Well, it was fun while it lasted, but it is nice to have the old place to ourselves again."

With that, he would slip quietly through his favourite hole in the hedge and amble off to see what the neighbour-hood had to offer. He might run across a pheasant's egg or two.. or even three.

In the meantime, however, the children's carefully dropped hints were finding an all-too-fertile soil in my head.

"I have been thinking.." I said.

This is invariably the cue for all the rest of the family to start looking alarmed.

"I have been thinking," I had said before I knocked a large hole in our suburban dining-room wall.

"I have been thinking," I had said, before I had ploughed up half the lawn and planted a forest of weeping-willows, rhododendron's and mile-high cupressi.

"I've been thinking," I had said, before I ripped out our best - rosebeds and dumped a swimming-pool into the hole.

"I've been thinking... about dogs."

There was an audible sigh of relief all round.

"If we cannot afford to keep any more of our own, why don't we offer to look after other people's and start a sort of kennels?"

They digested the idea in silence for a little while. It had its attractions, I could see, "Where would we put the kennels?" said Katherine rather apprehensively as she looked out of the window at what remained of the garden.

The "byres and barns"

"Well, in the field somewhere, we could.."

"Or in the vegetable-garden?"

"What would they look like?"

"Well, I've been to the library and got a few books out.." I always do. Libraries are my stand-by when I want to know anything. I discovered, not so long ago, that it runs in the family now. Katherine had just finished an impressive re-wiring of the old four-storeyed house she and her husband Doug had been renovating.

"How on earth did you know where all those wires went to?" I asked, wide-eyed with envy.

"Oh, it was easy, Mum," she replied. "I had this book out of the Library, you see..."

The books I had borrowed were full of dogs and full of kennels. They both came all shapes and sizes.

In fact there was only one thing all the kennels had in common: I couldn't find one that looked as though I could tap it together daintily in a leisurely afternoon. They were all man-size and obviously man- not womanmade and consisted of miles of chain-link netting (the expensive sort), mountains of concrete and forests of timber.

"I expect you would need planning permission, Mum," said sage Katherine after she had carefully looked through the first half dozen books. In the face of the prohibitive cost, that seemed the least of our worries, but it was a point.

"I need a licence, too."

"Gosh!" Even Elizabeth was impressed. "We are going to be official." We warmed to our plots and plans.

The next day I rang the RSPCA for the official ruling on our great idea. The little Inspector was charming. He would even run over and work it all out for me on the spot.

He leapt out of his car and re-designed all our out-buildings for me in ever such a short time. They were just right, he declared, and look, the runs could come right across the drive so, so, and so. I wasn't quite sure how we were going to get our car out of the garage when it had all been so beautifully constructed but he was so enthusiastic I felt convinced we could have easily tunnelled under the oak tree.. or perhaps under the railway!

"You must contact the local Sanitary Inspector," he added helpfully as he leapt back into his little car again, "He has the forms." Then he whizzed off in a whirlwind just like Elijah!

Next the Sanitary Inspector arrived. He was on our side too, it seemed.

He had a dog of his own, I learned later. It became one of our first boarders.

"No," he said. "You can't possibly have any kennels in the drive or in the buildings. They must go in the field."

I was sure he was right, all over again.

"Here are the forms and you will need three lots of

plans to submit to the Planning People."

It was very satisfying to have the actual forms in my hand. But I felt less and less competent to deal with the construction side. I needed to see a real Kennels in action. So taking the bull by the horns I rang up a large Kennels near Eastbourne and invited myself to a Royal Tour.

Dog-Town was fascinating, especially the block of brand-new runs. I could have happily curled up myself and bedded down with all those leaping, licking dogs in their centrally-heated luxury. The cost makes me shudder to think of it, even now. Perhaps if we could buy up a cement-works' take a degree in architecture and another in carpentry - and charge everybody in advance for the next ten years...

I was shown around the older runs that were temporarily empty. They looked a little down-at-heel. Well, you know what wood looks like when it has been standing out in the rain too long? Ten to one the dogs would have preferred them really, they love anything that has been standing out in the rain too long!

I was getting well-trained by now and I was extra careful to close the wire-mesh gate with a resounding clang behind us. My kind, long-suffering guide turned at the sound.

"Oh dear," she said philosophically, "'I am afraid you have locked us in. This one only opens from the outside." We were rescued in the end, but what with the dogs barking and us yelling.... However, it put a neat finishing touch to my education in dog-kennelling. Now I even knew it from the inside, from the point of view of the dogs.

Back home that evening we sat down to sketch our lay-outs.

"The pear-tree would give them a nice bit of shade."

"And drop all its leaves in the runs. No thank you."

"No, perhaps you're right. How about right over by the holly hedge, facing up to the house?"

"We could see what they were all up to then without having to actually go out in the rain."

"And get the full blast of their barking!" Their barking. Now that was something I had been firmly pushing right to the back of my mind ever since my tour of the Kennels.

I tried hard to make myself believe that our boarders wouldn't bark. But I knew jolly well that, with all day on their paws and nothing else to do, their favourite holiday-job would be to see who could bark the loudest and it seemed that at least one of the family was following my same train of thought.

"Remember that one next-door in Sanderstead?" she mused.

"The one that had to sit all day on the washing machine?"

"Yes, he never stopped barking.."

Goodness, I could hear him again, myself. His non-stop yapping had driven me, and every visitor we had, furious and frantic by turns for the miserable six months of his occupation.

I do believe, from that time on, I almost became allergic to barking altogether. I wasn't the only permanent victim, incidentally. At the end of the six months the husband, goaded presumably like myself beyond endurance, had marched the puppy out to an unknown destination for good - and himself as well.

But there must be an answer to it somewhere... and suddenly there was! We would not have our boarders cooped up in little runs where they were driven to noise out of sheer boredom, we would have them with us!

They would live in the house as our guests. Paying guests, that is. They would share our lives, they would curl up on our hearth-rug, they would share out meal-times, they would share our meals if they could, and life would be as full and exciting for them as it was for us.

So what need to bark? No time for it even.

They would never feel bored, lonely or neglected and our bonus would be that we should never have to go plodding out in the wind and the rain to feed and water them.

Moreover, miracles of miracles, our outlay was cut, overnight, from a thousand pounds worth of building materials to two or three rolls of chicken wire and a few dozen tent-pegs to make our garden dog-proof.

Goodness, it did seem easy!

Actually, we did plan for half-a-dozen cat-runs while we had all that paper in front of us. If we took in cats they would have to be enclosed, for obvious reasons. But we sited these also cosily in the garden so that we could all be one big, happy family.

Next day I posted off the forms and we considered ourselves in business. The World of Bureaucracy being what it is, the local council did not admit we were in business for a good five months more. However, in the meantime, it seemed sensible to have a few trial runs.

The word went round via the children and our friends. This corner of Sussex has a very well established bush-telegraph system, like all country districts. Some say it dates from the days of the smugglers when the barrels were hidden, en route, in Falmer pond, and I've no doubt in our Cooksbridge pond as well, until the word was passed round that the coast was clear and they could be hauled out, dripping, and sent on their way to London.

In comparison with the high-pressure salesmanship of modern advertising it may seem a rather tedious approach, to put the word around and just sit back and wait. But, after all, people who live in the country have based their business on the method since Joseph made his Pharaoh's fortune selling corn in Egypt.

Pass the word around and you never need a reference, too, it is in-built with the information. That's how we found it and a very important factor in this personal, guest-house business.

The reference works both ways, to vouch for, or to warn against. So if the voice at the other end of the phone shattered my ear drums with a domineering:

"This is Lady Hogweed speaking! My cousin has three Afghan Hounds... Yes, for tonight, of course...

Bonnie

You charge less when there are three I understand..?"

I knew the voice. I didn't even need to have the introduction bellowed down my ear. I knew how dreadfully her own, large dogs behaved when they came in to board and I remembered too how she sniffed with disapproval when it was time to pay the bill... So I was warned before she started her browbeating.

"No, I am sorry," I would answer as firmly as I could. "But we are full right up. Yes, until the end of next week.. and beyond.."

But if I met Bonnie's three owners, now it is a very different matter..

"We hope you won't be too cross but we have this

friend..." (They all talked together so you got the maximum of information the minimum of the time.) "Lives on her own and not too flush with money.." "But she loves her dog.." "It's very good at our house and we don't think it will give you any trouble.."

"We gave her your name just in case you had a vacancy for the last week in next month.."

And of course she's turned out gorgeous and perhaps, if she was hard up, we could lower the bill without her owner noticing.

So, as I say, in the beginning we plugged in on the local gossip-circuit and rang the curtain up on our first guest.

Looking back from the comforting vantage-point of so many years on, I wonder how we, or the poor house, even survived our very first season. Come to think of it, the garden suffered even more.

Every so often, I would announce, "Play time!" to our visitors. Then they would spit on their paws, roll up their sleeves and take a fast, bowler's run out into the hall and through the front-door. In a never failing, exuberant sea of waving tails and weaving noses they would hurl into the garden and scatter in all directions leaving me, helpless, on the door step.

Feeling like teacher-in-charge, I would fussily sprint this way and that, heading off each curious nose from the boundary netting or hurrying along a hopefully quivering hind leg from a new and vulnerable shrub.

After a wet day the hall carpeting looked more like the garden than the garden did itself.

"My," they would say to each other heartily as they were finally herded back into the house, "That toned me up a treat."

"A good shake now and I shall feel just dandy." You could easily tell at a glance which size of dog was in residence by the height, up the wallpaper, of the frieze of splattered mud.

Big dogs and Small dogs

In the sitting-room, the corners of all the arm-chairs became suspiciously damp and smelly and we learned fast that, where one leg was lifted, another invariably followed. We learned too that, in the kitchen, although our own dog was past the 'help yourself' stage, others were not nearly so far advanced. Butter, bacon, toast and even marmalade could disappear like magic. Sometimes it was more like boarding a litter of vacuum cleaners than a litter of dogs.

A few short, sharp lessons also taught us to close the larder door with military precision and never to estimate the height of a dog by what the tape measure said. Given enough incentives, one could sometimes add a good three feet or more!

In our initial eagerness to oblige, we accepted all creatures great and small. In the country, unfortunately, the great far outnumber the small. Our world seemed suddenly full of enormous Labrador's, Mastiffs or a fearsome mixture of the lot all packed in skillfully between a huge head and powerful tail.

Wonderful that we, or they, escaped alive. For, in the close quarters of our kitchen, where we all mostly lived, some of the larger dogs felt that their only chance of survival was to fight their way to Leader of the Pack by fair means or foul. One gigantic hound of the Baskerville's stood in the corner continually gnashing his fangs within inches of a gambolling pup, while, over against he Rayburn, our favourite, dainty, Yorkshire Terrier lady was snuggled up, blissfully asleep and completely concealed under the long fur of our own, peaceful mongrel.

Slowly we grew more circumspect as to whom we could safely welcome into our holiday home for dogs.

Regretfully we foreswore the largest boy dogs altogether and had to stipulate large bitches only. The bitches didn't seem to mind who was the leader of the pack however big they were. They just loved everybody, regardless and, if they were ultra-nervous to begin with, they just retired harmlessly to underneath a chair, growling softly, until the penny dropped that we loved them even if they were not too sure about them loving us.

Nearly always they soon became so much the other way inclined, that we were hard put to it to move across the kitchen floor without being bowled over by their constant deluges of affection.

Of course little dogs too, as Paddy had made it unforgettably clear, could start a fight just as expertly as the big dogs and usually a great deal faster.

"How on earth do you stop them?" our visitors used to ask, looking apprehensively at the dozens of paws padding busily around their feet.

It was the first process, as a family, we really perfected to a fine art - the breaking up of fights. We had to. It would have been awfully bad for business, after all, to have had to return a beloved pet to his doting Mum minus half an ear, or a champion booked for triumph at Crufts the following week heavily creased with unsightly scars.

Besides, fights upset everybody. They churn up the atmosphere, like a thunderstorm, and everybody's nerves go on jangling ages after the main shock has subsided.

We evolved a very smart bit of drill that we were justly proud of. At the first growl and answering shriek, each of us, where-ever we were and whatever we were doing, dropped everything and raced for the explosion.

Katherine would leave her transistor shouting the 'Beatles latest' to the void. Elizabeth would ditch her mice and Jenny would come running from the swing.

Then we all grabbed the nearest tail and PULLED

Fantastically, we were very seldom bitten and it always worked so well, I sometimes feel we ought to have had it patented. Only one drawback of course, some dogs don't have a tail. Not one of its original length, that is, because it has been docked, like a sheep's, at birth. It does seem unfair to the dog and equally unfair to us, but fortunately most of the breeds we took seemed to have had a good enough handful. And that's how we stopped the fights!

In the end we rarely had even a junior scrap. It wasn't so exciting for the family and our friends, but I found it much more restful. For one thing, we knew all the dogs who came to stay with us very well. They mostly all came regularly, even if it was only once a year while Mum and Dad made their annual pilgrimage to the sun.

We knew the way their minds worked and we had acquired a sort of 'unconscious ear' for what they were planning almost before they knew about it themselves. It was not a sixth sense, it is just that we noticed that they helpfully doled out clues the whole time, like a twitch of the ear and a wary cock of the head or a low, 'invitation' growl.

Also they all had their own individual reasons for a scrap. Sometimes they just felt like putting an uppish new-comer in his place. They knew instinctively who needed the treatment and who didn't. They could have done it just as well by growling but perhaps they felt that a short, sharp pounce made their point that much more effective.

The Terrier breeds were the ones who indulged the most. They just adored rolling up their sleeves for a fine old rough and tumble. It aided their digestion and stretched their little legs. They danced delightedly around each other, making enormous growls and barks, because it was their idea of fun.

And so it was, as long as all the others did not spoil it by joining in and that some dogs just can't resist. Even the bitches succumbed to the temptation when the pace got really hot. But as long as the fighters were basically good tempered, you could reason with them much more easily than people realise. One Cairn, called Stavros, now, who came to stay, presented himself with an important air of complete self- possession when he arrived from London, where he lived. He was beautifully stripped and groomed and flatteringly delighted to be with us. He oozed with charm and with good manners.

In fact, he was sizing up every available sparing partner in the room and his little heart was beating fast with all the pleasures of anticipation.

Throwing off his Town manners, he launched joyfully into the fray, open to allcomers and (if nobody took up his challenge, he might even be tempted to throw himself, happily, on the nearest dog available and 'make a meal' of him.

But, funnily enough, he meant no harm and he knew, as we knew, that fighting was not allowed. So we had an unwritten agreement that, fun over, he would allow himself to be firmly plonked back into his sensible basket and the wire mesh latched across. There he could sit, subdued but suitably triumphant, and honours were considered even on all sides.

Dogs for Tea

CHAPTER V

DOGS AND MORE DOGS

All our guests from Town fortunately did not pack quite so much of the fury of the Norsemen in their luggage as Stavros did, Benjie, who looked a cross between a Schnautzer and a Scottie, brought his own, personal, party trick of being able to twirl like a Dancing Dervish when life inspired him to it. It was a lot less aggressive in its fury although it stirred the dust up on the kitchen floor in much the same way.

Well, you couldn't charge extra for stirred up dust any more than you for scratched-off paint. Indeed, sometimes I think we gave double value for the hidden advantages of our sort of family boarding, especially with the dogs who did not go places and meet people very much.

"Its splendid! Twiggy is not nearly so shy since she stayed with you last Easter."

"Cindy used to always growl at strangers when we met them, but now she never seems to mind at all."

We shouldn't have taken the credit for it really,

though it was tempting, because it was not so much us, as the whole system, that got the good results. Just like sending your only child to boarding-school and a lot less expensive.

Yet, with some, even we had to admit defeat. Especially with gentlemen Spaniels. Not the King Charles varieties since they have a long heritage of highly civilised pet-life behind them, but those amiable, adoring-eyed Springers and Cockers. They love humans and they do so want humans to love them, they make devoted pets in their own homes. But out of their accustomed element and sharing a kitchen with so many strangers, they were ultra-suspicious, ultra-sensitive and incredibly unpopular with every dog in sight.

They remind me, more than anything, of aged military gentlemen, forced by circumstances to retire to the faded dullness of a small boarding-house. They live still in their dreams of regimental glory. The harness still jangles in the eastern sunlight. The cavalry still sweeps across the scorching

The King Charles - always one of the family

plain. And so they grumble and rumble their twilight years away, aching to be active and vigorous once more, to breath the air of youth and the great outdoors.

Just so did the Spaniels growl and mutter as they paced restlessly around the kitchen. Or they sat in their beds, barking irascibly at every dog in view. Their whiskers sprouting with annoyance and frustration.

They are sporting dogs, you see. Bred for the open, working life, following the gun and marking down the prey. Outside they could tolerate a companion dog, they were too busy snuffling around at their own important duties, to trouble about them very much. But inside, they neither loved their fellow boarders nor were loved by them.

Even the gorgeous-coated Clumber Spaniel was no exception and he was the odd man out for the whole of his stay and a source of bad-temper and ill-feeling all round.

Beagles too, we soon found, made uncomfortable guests. So many of them have an inborn urge to roam as far as possible in the shortest possible time. Since they had all day on their paws to find, or make, a suitable weak spot in the fencing as a starter, I could have done with a set up of anti-theft television cameras, chain-store fashion, to keep an eye on their successes.

I remember one Summer, not long after we had started the kennels, we spent a glorious fortnight in the

Lake District and were delighted to discover the yard of the local Beagle Pack just along the valley. We promptly fell in love with them as they all leapt and gambolled in the sunshine.

A glorious fortnight in the Lake District

Their brown eyes were warm with affection and their long, silky ears and puppy-like paws completely won our hearts. We even bought a small, china family, complete. It stands on our Welsh-dresser to this day.

But when I rang our vet and mentioned that the Beagle was, from now on, the dog of our hearts desire, I was quite taken aback by his vehement reply.

"It isn't, you know," he fired back, firmly, down the phone.

"If you want to spend the rest of your life combing the neighbourhood for your pet," he said, "Buy a Beagle by all means."

"If you want a dog that will be the most difficult to train to obedience and good manners, go right ahead..."

And I found later, much to my surprise, that he was right. No boy Beagle ever boarded with us who was a non-barker, a non-stealer or a nonroamer. They were fun. They were loveable - but deafening, and we were always awfully glad to see them all go home!

At first, with our very amateur line in netting, it was one enormous headache making sure we were always one leap ahead of the dogs who had the in-built wanderlust. Conversely, some whose owners had handed them over with ominous fore-bodings of incurable route-march habits, turned out to be quite the laziest and most home-loving guests you could find.

When she was in her own home now, dear old Prim, the Labrador, used to heave herself out of her basket late on in the morning, give herself a good shake and mutter under her breath,

"Well, time I took my stroll down to the 'Roebuck' at Laughton for a quick one. Good company there at lunch time and the home-made pate takes a bit of licking."

With all the boys at boarding-school it was pretty quiet around the house and down at the Local, she always found a tasty welcome with lots of cheerful company thrown in.

If she had put her mind to the problem of getting through our initial chicken-wire when she stayed with us, she could have disappeared daily in the direction of our Local too, any time she wanted. Instead she would open one sleepy eye, survey the other half-dozen inmates of the kitchen contentedly and snuggle down to another forty-winks before the gong for lunch at twelve O'clock. After that, it just wasn't worth the effort. Besides, she might miss the free carrots that came when I was getting the dinner.... and then there were the supper titbits...

But other boarders were not so amiable.

When Miss Blaker brought her large, brown Dachshund she would say, "I am so happy that he is staying with you, dear. I feel he is going on his holiday too and

Always ready for a game

will enjoy it every bit as much as I will mine. Such a lovely boy."

But Rufus was not nearly the docile gentleman that he looked. At home, he ruled the household with an iron paw, slept on the best bed, ate the choicest meat and had a devoted retinue of unmarried slaves.

"Huh," he would grumble, after the taxi, "A bit below my style, this place. Sharing a bedroom with a crowd of other dogs! Well, I'd better let them know just who I am and what I think of them."

He glowered at the company who sniffed him cheerfully and told him he was much too fat.

"Too fat, indeed. I'll show you!"

He slid outside and ambled innocently along the path into the paddock. There he made a thorough assessment of the boundaries, spotted the weakest wire and went to work....

Having got out, he gave himself an enormous pat on the back and huffed and puffed his way along the road and down the drive again, barking sardonically.

"How's that then? Said I would teach you, didn't I? Now try and keep me in."

He stayed with us every year from then until he died and every year he spent the total waking minutes of his stay patrolling the boundaries, yard by yard, to prove his superiority.

It was his constant success that taught us how strong and penetrating the snout of a really determined dog can be. The dachshunds are tailor-built for tackling one-inch mesh and their sharp teeth make mincemeat of chicken wire in far less time than it takes me with a pair of wire-cutters.

Though what Rufus really needed was, not stronger fencing, but a sense of humour. Most dogs have one and it makes them, like humans, so much easier to get on with.

However, some can have too much...

Take Zebedee now, the Labrador who came to stay with Tig the Long-haired Dachshund.

Zebedee was one who felt life was for living and for fun and, gosh, coming to stay with all these dogs was his idea of going to the Ball. He had so many bright ideas he's rather like an Elizabeth with four legs and a tail.

"Tell you what," he would bark to Tiggy, "How about you and me having this game of digging? See who can be the first through to Australia.

Goodness, this ground is hard. Perhaps we should get the Lurchers (Caraway and Dill) to help."

You would think they were, all four, going pot-holing they dug so deep. When the rabbits took over from the moles and scrabbled their tunnels under the railway chain-link fence, Zebedee had his greatest idea yet.

"My, rabbits! How delicious! And that burrow runs right through. I am sure they made them just for me to follow.

A garden for dogs

"Oh too small. Now that's a pity. Still, not too small for Tiggy..."

He padded off in search of Tig.

"Want to catch some rabbits, Tig? Good, I'll show you how its done." He led him to the biggest tunnel. Tiggy, nothing loath, pranced after him.

"Now see that hole there?" He nosed it out and scrabbled it big enough to fit round Tiggy's tum. "See if you can push through now. You can? Hey, that's terrific. Who is the cleverest then?"

Poor Tiggy, emerging on the other side into the railway ditch, was not too sure.

"Where do I go from here?" he yelped.... no further, luckily, as it is the electrified Main Line to London. Retrieving him was not so much fun either, the fence was topped, at six-feet, with barbed wire, three strands of it.

But Zebedee's so pleased with his good ideas you could not be cross with him for long.

The railway fence bordered the south side of the paddock to where we had long since re-directed the dogs instead of having them share our flower garden. So much for our original idealism of, "We'll all enjoy life much more as one great, big, happy family."

After I had lost my third Ceanothus, at two pounds a time, practically all the border-plants and roughly half the lawn, it did seem time to re-think the playtime plans.

"We could plant toy umbrellas all around the flower beds," suggested small Jenny, helpfully. It was a fascinating thought and might have looked even prettier than when Elizabeth tied the artificial roses all along the trellis, but I felt that something more effective still was needed.

So we opened up a new doorway to the outside, from the kitchen, this time leading into the paddock and netted off the garden altogether. Now the dogs had a quarter of an acre of meadow all to themselves and they had it ever after. They could play hide-and-seek and Chase-me-Charlie to their hearts content. They could sit and think in the sunshine... or they could just plain sit! Plenty of room for everybody and probably as much a relief to them as it was to us.

On their side of the netting, the border plants were happy too. Now they could dare to open their eyes without the inevitable blast of liquid poison they had come to dread. Of course the weeds cashed in on it as well, especially the stinging-nettles who honestly think they own the place. I found

I had traded the hours spent in looking after the dogs, with at least an equal time in pulling up all the nettles that had moved in to take their place.

My gardening book says, "Nettles are a sign of high fertility!" Which is meant to be encouraging, I am sure, only the nettles here had a good look over my shoulder when I was reading that page and promptly took it to mean that it was high fertility specifically for them. They worked on that ever after. Their nursery-bed was in the strawberries. They had outlying colonies in every flower-bed and their thriving capital was in the shrubbery.

But the dogs enjoyed my sessions of nettle-warfare enormously. They lined-up on the other side of the netting and laid loud bets on which side they are backing to win.

"She's winning! Look, there's another armful down!"

"Come on, Angie," shouts Rosie.

"Hi there, Bonnie, you're missing all the fun!"

They leaped up and down in their enthusiasm, it almost made me feel I was worth watching and they barked most encouraging commentaries on the day's play.

"Bet you that one stings her when she is not looking. Oops," Bark, bark, "What did I say, then.?"

"Race you round the field," yapped Ginty, the Terrier, while she stops for a breather. "Oh my. The language."

But there is one thing about dogs. They really are a wonderful boost to your morale even in the most trying circumstances.

Returning to the kitchen and its alterations... We had added an extra door to the room, as I have said, so it seemed a good idea to block up one of the others. It still left us with the original quota of four, which was quite enough for the dogs to scratch at and enough for me to have had to repaint when decorating time came round.

The door we blocked off was the one that led directly into the drive and we extended the working top across it to give a nine-foot length inside the room. Outside, it made the comings and goings safer, for now everybody entering from the drive had to negotiate the wash-house before they arrived at the kitchen and there was no danger now of a dog casually walking out as the humans were walking in.

The space under the working top we divided into three divisions with wood and hardboard and, hey presto. Three alcoves for three dog-bedrooms. In the corner, over by the Rayburn, was a built-in cupboard from floor to ceiling. This only needed the door and inside shelf taking away to reveal yet another cosy corner for a boarder. And so it went on. . .

The dogs brought their own beds and bedding. The owners didn't usually know it but every new bed was considered fair game by all the other dogs in residence, especially the permanent ones. Hardly had the visiting car rolled off than the first in the queue had dropped itself neatly into the latest arrival's bed.

Poodles bring luxury beds

"How do you think it suits me?" she would smuggly enquire of the envious line of would-be occupants.

"A little large at the tail end, perhaps?

She would sniff under the spotless blankets.. and sniff again and produce, in interesting succession, a rubber ball, a half-chewed bone and, bingo, two biscuits. It was always worth heading the queue for the latest bed.

Like the dogs themselves, their beds came in all shapes and sizes. I had a bonus from a luscious Standard poodle's dog-bed once. We were full to overflowing and the afternoon sun was flooding in. Since two dogs had already commandeered the only comfortable chair, I sat down on this luxurious dog divan, complete with its own king-size, foam-rubber mattress. In no time, my head was down as well and I was fast asleep for the next hour while all the big dogs mounted guard around me.

The kitchen floor of Sussex brick we did not have to change. It stood up manfully to the army of ever-padding feet. It needed its face washing a couple of times a day in the height of the season... and a couple of times an hour if we happened to be full in the mud of winter.

Our vacuum-cleaner was almost as long-suffering as the floor. It had to be. If only one could do something with all that fur. Some dogs discard it faster than the Dance of the seven Veils.

But the medal for 'Bravery and Devotion to Duty under Constant Fire', that went without hesitation, to the family.

There was Katherine now, who used to climb me, like a lamp-post, in terror, at every approaching Poodle when she was knee-high. She and her Doug refitted the kitchen like magic for us and the dogs one Sunday afternoon and, guess what their first buy was when they settled down to married bliss? Yes, an Alsatian.

Next to food, what the dogs love best in the world is being the centre of somebody's loving and undiluted attention. This was naturally where Elizabeth always came in.

It wasn't so easy when I was there on my own through the day, to make every one of, say, eight or ten dogs feel that each was the apple of my eye. But when Elizabeth came breezing in from school and exclaimed delightedly.

"Oh hallo, Rocky! Oh good, Cindy's come!"

You should have seen how all the tails would start to beat up the dust and how all twenty ears would prick up in answer to the cheerful lilt in her voice. It was just like somebody switching on the light. The whole room suddenly woke up and rejoiced! She had added her own contribution to the kennels years before, needless to say.

"Mummy I must have a dog to take for walks on Sunday!"

Funny, I had not even noticed her going for walks on any day, let alone on Sundays.

"No, but I should if I had a dog to take!"

Nobody has ever bettered Elizabeth at convincing quick-fire explanations. I looked round helplessly at the assortment of dogs at her disposal but I knew

Jemima

that I was beaten before I started, Elizabeth had already arranged it...

She soon arrived home happily cradling a small, fat and very apprehensive puppy in her arms. It mushroomed into the busiest, bounciest Golden Labrador ever invented -and, that's saying something!

She shrieked the house down at every feeding time. She shouted, "Thieves! Murder! Fire!" whenever anybody even tapped on the back-door and she daily manufactured and scattered as much loose fur as Mother Goose providing her snow-storm. She was Jemima, originally with the 'Puddle-duck' attached to it before she became house-trained, and she was Elizabeth's pride and joy.

Elizabeth has, long ago, convinced everybody else that Jemima's their pride and joy too. She has a husband now, Steve, and Jemima is, of course, his pride and joy as well.

But then she had foresightedly set him on the path of animal ownership, from the first, by endowing him with a hamster by way of an engagement present!

In the end, Jenny was the only one left of the children to give me daily encouragement and support. In her quiet, gentle way, she had grown even more zoo-minded than all the rest of us put together. She always was the best at actually handling the dogs and she had manfully taken on the job of providing the varied succession of livestock that Elizabeth always considered so essential to our family life.

Hamsters, guinea-pigs, rabbits and there was far worse to come which I will tell you all about when we have finished with the dogs. Her latest then, was a super Golden Retriever - that's Toffee, who helped Zebedee in his search for oil and Australia.

She was as quiet and gentle as Jemima-cousin was loud and boisterous but she was great fun and just like Jenny.

Last but not least, there was Keith who provided house and home for us all and never, in his wildest dreams, envisaged himself as head Gamekeeper for Animal-Farm-come true.

He ostensibly left the intricacies of zoo keeping to us, weaker sex, and steered a careful, middle path between his job in town and his unconventional home life. But you should have seen the attentive circle of hopeful faces that surrounded him when he was eating his supper every evening. The entertainment he provided, in the shape of crusts and rinds, was quite obviously far more absorbing than the most thrilling bed-time tale.

Two familiar faces

CHAPTER VI

AND YET MORE DOGS

It used to be a standing joke in our family when I was young that wherever you went out with my mother, who had been a teacher, she was sure to be able to point out a passer-by whom she had taught as a girl

"Oh Mum," we would cry, "Not another!"

In the end I became just as incorrigible. Everywhere I went I passed this dog whom I had boarded or that lady whose cat had come to stay. I'm beginning to think it must be a family failing.

Two awe-inspiring windows in Lewes town

Still it was rather fun to look up at two awe-inspiring windows in Lewes town and be barked at cheerfully by two familiar bearded faces.

"'Hoots," they would shout in their best Scots accent, because Rosie and Patty were Scottish Terriers you see, "If you'll just step inside there'll be a wee cup of something for you, for sure now..."

I like to think they said it just for me, though I knew darned well they spent all day barking out the same invitation to everyone who passed. Still, it was fun.

We had even reached the stage of welcoming some of their children's children! We had our fair share of puppies. I think I was getting the tiniest bit jaundiced about them in the end, they were so expensive to have around, especially with mats and cushions.

Sometimes I think their owners felt as though they were giving us a big treat, looking after their 'small angel'...

"He is only dirty at night!" . . .'

Or, "He likes chewing a bone at bedtime..." Huh, you can just see us giving him a bone, all to himself, at bedtime. It would cause a riot! Think of it, eight dogs and one bone!

Eight dogs and eight bones probably wouldn't work, either. Somebody would always covet the bone next door. It is not only with humans that the grass is greener on the other side of the fence. So instead of a bone, puppy would probably devote most of his first hours of darkness to one of the chair or table legs, egged on, no doubt, by a very chatty circle of admirers.

"Cor, wish we had the nerve!"

"Good work, young fella, keep it up!"

"At it Junior! You are a one!"

And, if the night in question happened to have been

the one before Elizabeth or Jenny's O Levels, you could have heard my Lesson 1 in Hotel Behaviour for Puppies very clearly - right at the end of our drive!

Fortunately the older dogs were surprisingly tolerant of a young pup bouncing them for six at an unexpected moment and it learnt quickly. So it usually went home a good deal more grown up than it came in. The same applied to the very pampered pets who arrived demanding,

"Where's my special this.." and "Where's my extra that..?" and growl nastily when Toffee offered to try out their bed for size. Within a week, like Friday's Child, they had metamorphosed into quite respectable loving and giving creatures, only we often had to do it all over again when they came in the next time...

The elderly dogs now, they could be rather a responsibility too and, charming as they usually were, it was an extra relief to be able to deliver them back to their owners in the same condition in which they arrived. Because, after all, in an Ark like ours, with eight or ten dogs on board, anything could happen. Our rule was to treat our guests exactly as we treated our own. It was the only way.

The Elderly dog

Mind you, the very old dog who led a rather too quiet and sedately solitary existence with his quiet, sedate and elderly owners shed a good five years once he entered into the spirit of things. One old gentleman Cairn who had been the Muhammad Ali of his neighbourhood in his time (and who also, incidentally, had the unfortunate habit of backing-up against a stone when he did his duty and thus carried a good chunk of it away, squashed onto him) he was invariably handed over with a, "Now dear, don't hesitate to attend to everything if you feel he should be taken to the Vet."

What she meant was, "I do feel he is a little bit of a trial now but it is so hard to know when I ought to have him put to sleep.."

She was a very sensible, kindly, lady and we did sympathise with her. Unfortunately her 'trial' used to take on a new lease of life from the minute that she left him with us. All those girls around enchanted him hugely, he was an honest rake at heart, and the proximity of all the boys gave him heavenly recollections of his former battle-honours. He always went home in enormous form and years further from his natural end than ever..

I used to feel almost apologetic.

You would like to hear about the doyen of our establishment in his time, I know. The guest to end all guests. To look at he was the saddest, most. mournful animal you could possibly imagine. His head hung low. His ears dangled to the floor and his gigantic paws plodded gloomily underneath him with an elephantine gait. It was not until well after his first visit (it usually was) that we learned how he terrorised his folks at home, anointing the choicest drapes and furnishings imperiously regardless of all remonstrance. He would even occupy the double bed, when he got the chance, and hold it with terrifying growls against all corners - especially his owner's husband!

He wasn't very old but his knowledge of human nature was uncannily mature and, as he was the twin image of the current television advertisement for suede shoes, we immediately re-christened him 'Hush-pup'.

Perhaps he felt the name suited him better than his elegant, pedigree title of Cholmodely. He accepted it with tolerant grace and prowled restlessly around the chairs and the table growling provocatively at the world in general.

Yes, he cocked his leg firmly at every corner to establish his dominance. He also took liberties with all the girls and tried to bully all the rest of us. It was a very impressive performance. It impressed us enormously at first. We were fairly new to the game at the time. Try as I could, I found it difficult to get on what you might call 'affectionate terms' with this hard, unhappy chunk of leather and bone. 'Hard' was the operative word certainly. When you patted him, your hand came back to you a lot more bruised and battered than it went out. It was like caressing a frame of solid iron - well, it was solid bone, after all. And not for nothing are the ears of the Basset Hound known, in the trade, as 'leathers'. Nothing soft and furry and loveable about them. There they drooped, long, lean and cold, nine inches of unadorned hide dangling to the floor.

He eventually sat himself down, thump, in the best place of course, on the mat in front of the Rayburn. He was resigned to his fate!... when, all of a sudden, a large blue-bottle buzzed in through the garden-door.

Hush-pup leaped to his massive feet and his ears did a series of colossal somersaults as his head whirled here and there after the buzzing fly. He forgot all about his cherished role of down-trodden martyr in the hectic excitement of the moment. His mournful eyes sparkled with puppy delight as he gambolled the length and breadth of the kitchen, jumping, cavorting, bounding here, bounding there, bounding everywhere!

A good thing our furniture was mostly tubular metal or solid oak and our floor good Sussex brick, because all fifty pounds of Hush were bouncing up and down on it like a steam-hammer.

However, all told, it was the biggest give-away of the season. Suddenly Hush became a nice, normal, ordinary dog with, hidden away between those long ears, a gorgeous sense of humour and likableness. Suddenly, too, we understood his language quite plainly. His growls meant, "I feel a bit shy and I'm trying to cover it up with this super noise so that everybody will be very frightened of me until I feel more at home."

His puddles here and puddles there had rather the same message but were meant particularly to impress the other boy-dogs in residence. We found later that, when we attached him to a long piece of string, it made him feel safe so then he didn't have to puddle at all to establish himself. It saved a lot of cleaning...

It turned out that he just adored playing with the other dogs and he would race round and round the field, like a brown and white cannon-ball, shouting his head off with joyful excitement. We didn't mind his shouting at that distance, but to get the full blast of it at close quarters was a pretty shattering experience. He had, of course, his own impossible bark that started as an immense rumble, like an impending earthquake, somewhere deep down inside him. Then it slowly and remorselessly gathered strength as it rose to the surface until the gigantic blast of it came booming out of his jaws.

He put all he had into his bark, did Hush, and many is the cup of tea I have seen spilt by people on the receiving end of it! He also loved lying on his back with his white fur uppermost and his great paws dangling helplessly to have his tummy tickled. It was for all the world like tickling the breast of the Christmas turkey (with less meat on it) for Hush was as much all-bone underneath as he was on top. Still, we did our best with what facilities he offered..

On his first visits he spent a good deal of his time and energy trying to prove his superiority by making mince-meat of our wire-netting. He had the hardest nose of any dog I have ever come across and the toughest paws for digging, too. So, what with a built-in bull-dozer, wire-cutters disguised as teeth, and two hefty shovels, he took some keeping in. Besides, at home he could wander far and wide at will, so it was obviously a matter of personal pride to him to establish the same terms for himself on holiday.

However, he soon began to enjoy himself so much (and. no doubt the fencing also improved) that he decided it was too comfortable to bother about leaving. So he settled down to the best corner of the kitchen instead and rose to be quite a commendable visitor in our establishment.

But his owners were elderly and Hush, at home, was as big a trial as ever. So a new home was found for him about three miles away. Hush transferred homes amiably enough but became confused all of a sudden. First he would turn up at one house and then suddenly he would be found sitting on the doorstep of the other house. The new and old owners got confused as well.

In fact, he tied them up in knots so much that eventually he had to be restored to his first home.

Then he thought up an even more interesting routine. One night I was woken up, at about midnight, by a gruesome scratching and whining sound in the front garden. It was Master Hush trying his hardest to bore a way through our front door!

Easy enough to just open the door and let him in you may think. But wait. In the kitchen are eight more dogs all peacefully asleep in their baskets and every corner full and just try introducing a stranger into that lot without waking up the whole household, humans included! Why, it often took me a solid hour of patient cajoling to get a new arrival accepted in broad daylight and with a whole field at my disposal!

All round it wasn't a too popular turn of events and I was thankful, in the morning, to return him to his Mum again.

But there was no stopping his Lordship after that. Next time he made for the back kitchen-door.. and the next... But in time I decided to put a stop to my broken nights and left him in the porch until morning. He fell in with this arrangement surprisingly intelligently and agreed to bed-down in the back-porch on arrival and not to disturb us until getting-up time.

Winter came on and I felt sure that the cold and the wet would confine him to barracks and perhaps, by the time Spring arrived, his wanderlust would have been forgotten. . . .

There speaks Old Hopeful again!

He lived all of six miles away and a busy London road covers most of it, but through snow and pouring rain Hush-pup still made his nocturnal pilgrimage. We weren't the only ones he visited. It was just that when he arrived here he invariably stayed, so we were the only resting point discoverable. It became almost a habit with me to ring up his mistress at breakfast-time and he would wait philosophically for his transport to draw up before booming his way happily off for the drive home.

Worried that he should get a chill or rheumatism in his solid chunk of bone, we put a large nest of straw in the open garage which he then amenably curled up into on his late arrival. This was a much more satisfactory arrangement from our point of view as it did not disturb the dogs inside the kitchen who could often scent a stranger in the porch, however quiet he was.

So Hush then waited tolerantly in his bed of straw for his morning taxi home and sometimes I didn't even have to ring... the car came automatically!

With the better weather, it seemed even more convenient and agreeable if we tied him up at the top of the drive to sit on the grass, in the sun, to await his transport.

Believe it or not, but after two sessions of that, we went out, one morning, to find our self-invited and very self-possessed Hush sitting himself, with lordly elegance, on the grass exactly at the end of the drive, confidently anticipating his car home with as much aplomb as a business executive awaiting his London train on Lewes Station.

He was obviously a Basset in a thousand. The only other Basset Hound we had been on close terms with was not a patch on Hush. He was an extremely ill-tempered gentleman with very few manners and no sense of humour.

Sometimes I allow myself to fancy that Hush was a shy, jolly, little puppy who, by an unfortunate over-sight at 'Headquarters' had been incarnated into the wrong skin. And thus burdened with the awesome weight of a Basset Hound carcass, his pilgrimage through life was as ponderous and frustrating as his melancholy eyes portrayed.

Under the circumstances, I guess he romped over the finishing-line to a very understanding round of applause in the Other World. After all, it isn't what you are, it is what you MAKE of what you are that counts - even with dogs!

Hush-Pup

CHAPTER VII

WHICH SHALL WE CHOOSE

People who flatteringly think we know far more about dogs than we really do, often ask us, "Which breed of dog, do you think, is the best to have?" It is the sort of question like, How would you spend Seventy thousand pound Pools or Lottery win? that I can spend happy hours dreaming over. Added to which, since I always forget the answer as soon as I have arrived at it, I have the enjoyment of going through the whole process of deduction again the next time somebody asks.

It really is a process of deduction, too, in that you count out the breeds in turn as you remember their individual dis-advantages .

Working dogs I would rule out straight away, unless you can provide them with the exercise and responsibility they need. Labrador's, Sheep-dogs, Alsatians and the larger hounds all come into this category.

One owner of several Alsatians we heard of recently, has hit on the brilliant idea of training his dogs to the daily task of bringing up all the logs for the fires, each day, from the large pile stacked right at the bottom of the garden. They bring them in single mouthfuls and place them tidily at the back door for use and are as happy as sandboys, out of mischief and as pleased as punch at fulfilling their own, personal responsibility.

Elizabeth's uproarious Labrador was always tickled pink by her one achievement of rocketing up the drive to bring back the daily paper from the front gate. She would prance back with it in her mouth like a winning Derby favourite but alas, we had only one paper each day, the rest of the day could be rather trying!

Despite their endearing and good-natured temperament, I rule out Labrador's as the ideal in any case because, like Jemima, most of them shed enough fur, day in and day out, to fill an endless chain of Continental quilts. I can't think where they manufacture it all: You can brush it out, comb it out and even vacuum-clean it out, yet, while you turn round to put the cleaner back into its corner, one shake and the floor is knee-deep in dog hairs all over again.

Katherine and Toffee

They do seem to love riding in cars though. Jermima would have lived in one if she could. So if you live in your car and want a constant companion - providing you never wear black or navy-blue and are not asthmatic - a Labrador might be your cup of tea, after all.

Our favourite of the moment, for us, is the Golden-Haired Retriever because Jenny's Toffee was so beautiful and good, as is her present Retriever, Parsley.

They are picture dogs, you must agree, and practically self-cleaning. They share their fur around as liberally as the best, but then, they share their love and their undying loyalty with it. Peaceful and fun, they are one of the easiest breeds to train as they are so even-tempered and intelligent.

When you come to list them all, what a great number of breeds of dog there are around now to choose from and, what appeals to one, may be anathema to another.

Whippets and Lurchers now, they either brighten your life, like the rising sun, or they never raise a spark. You either find their sleekness dreamily lithe and elegant or you look on it as a skin-tight bag of bones which hurts your hand every time you forget and give it a resounding pat.

If you yearn to own a Whippet or a Lurcher, do not be taken in by their apparent size. Some of them look quite small even though they may actually stand higher than a Sheep Dog. Their slenderness is deceptive. Added to which they all have the ability, and the liking, to rear up gracefully on their hind legs and wave two long, feeler-like, front paws in front of your chest or, alternatively, over the kitchen table. They do have long, needle-sharp claws, too!

We classed them firmly as large dogs, for their capacity for food is as large as that of a Labrador and that is saying something. Sometimes, indeed, it seems like pouring food down a bottomless drain as the Whippet never seems to get fat on it. But to his owner it is a very precious drain. Whippet owners, without exception, are the most devoted owners in the world.

Another very special breed, in our eyes, was the Pekinese. I love them still. Before I had met them, to be on actual speaking terms, that is, I can remember to my shame how I compared them, not too complimentarily, to 'something between a dog and a cat'.

Perhaps, on further acquaintance, I was not so far out after all. They are certainly a rather specialised sort of dog. Perhaps they ought to have a species all to themselves, Dogs, Cats and Pekinese (with their allied breed, the ShiTzu).

Whatever they are, they are fun. They have an enormous sense of humour and an I.Q. which is streets ahead of some humans I know and a colossal inbred sense of the fitness of things. They will romp and play like, or with, a kitten but always, when the occasion demands, they can re-assume their dignity as naturally and as easily as the Imperial Presence they once embellished. For royal dogs they are, whether they are lording it at Crufts or snuffling out a beetle on the kitchen floor.

I love their long, silky coats and the furious sweeping of their tails to indicate their displeasure when affronted. Yes, they do get into tangles and they do bring in half the garden at times, but they are easily brushed and combed and repay the treatment a hundredfold.

I think, myself, they are just as attractive with some of the excess of fur trimmed off. All very well to trail all that extravagance across the inlaid floors of the Royal Pagoda but, when promenading on good old Wealden clay, it is quite a different matter and two inches of fur, attached to each paw, becomes two inches of black mud in no time at all. One has to be practical, even with Pekes.

But if I were a Pekinese breeder, my biggest aim in life would be to breed a really recognisable nose on the end of that poor little squashed-in-face. That would be a true kindness to repay all the loyalty and joy they give. They might look less like oriental portraits but they would be much healthier, happier dogs.

I always threatened the family that I shall finally retire in the company of two, black Pekes. Retire from work, I mean, not for the night. For, as bed companions, they leave a lot to be desired. They snore!

So do King Charles Spaniels among others. One of our visitors could be heard through two walls and a floor. Which is reminiscent of the first hamster cage we had with its wheel attached. Hamsters are nocturnal, unfortunately, and the drumming of that wheel could be heard through two floors!

And now for the ideal dog.

The most all-round success of the dogs we had boarded, we had found, was the long-haired Dachshund. Brown or, black, they are both very good looking, gentle but fun, endlessly sporting, clean and intelligent.

They have a silky fur, which appears to be pretty well self-cleaning and self-trimming and which always looks attractive. They have an appealing face at the front end and the back view is a great improvement on most other breeds.

They are not as jumpy as the Terriers and not so delicate as the Spaniels but are game for whatever you are game for. They do not grow as large, or nearly so heavy, as the ordinary Dachshund and they do have that delightful ability to relax in complete peace when their owner feels that way too.

So there you are, for what it is worth, our rating of the nearest one can get to the ideal dog!

I always think that it is a pity that there is not some sort of borrowing system where dog ownership is concerned. It is so difficult to know which is the right breed for, you until you have chosen the wrong one... and then it is too late. For don't we all get much too easily carried away into realms of rapture at the sight of all those plump, wriggling, furry babies, quite forgetting that the odds are that they could mushroom into headstrong Pandas in less than twelve months?

Still, a dog can live for anything up to eighteen or so years, so if you ever find yourself saddled with the sort of dog who just isn't your cup of tea, however hard you try, my advice is, Advertise! Just that! Put an advertisement in the local paper,

"Good home wanted..." then a few, reasonably truthful details and you will certainly be able to pick a really first-class alternative home for the dog and save yourself, and probably the dog too, years of torture. Don't feel guilty about it either. It is a pity some people did not do it ages ago!

When you think of it, it could be a lot better if we could do the same with unwanted children! All those children one hears about, starved and beaten and wanting so much to be loved and needed and all those childless couples aching for a family... One can do a lot worse than be a dog with a 'dog's life' these days.

I suppose every animal owner, once in their life, may meet up with one that seems in some way more than just an animal. A fox or an otter, say, in the wild, or a horse like Arkle, a donkey... or a dog! One that seems to share an extra intelligence and to have an almost human understanding.

Even with all the dogs and cats that have come and

gone through our doors here, I can count the extra special ones on one hand and still have fingers to spare. But the first one of all of them was - Lucy!

We did not adopt her, she bounced in, at six months, and knew from the minute that I had picked her up from her previous owners that this was her home for life, even if we didn't. I was not all that struck on Dachshunds at the time and she was a small, black Dachshund, as thin as a rake and painfully shy. But she did have the delightful name of Lucy and she did have the loveliest head and the silkiest, black ears that a Dachshund ever had.

Her eyes were her best feature. They were brown and melting and sparkling by turns. Yes, of course I was a proud Mum so you don't have to believe me. But we

"Granny"

do have a beautiful blue rosette to prove it. Our only rosette too, in the dog line. Won for being the dog with the most appealing eyes... It was just up Lucy's street.

She hated the Dog Show more than anything she had hated in her life before. She just wanted to go home. So she sat there in the line up and raised her graceful head to the judge and appealed, with all her canine radar, "Please can I go home?

Quick, quick, quick..." ... and won the rosette!

The only trouble about being blessed with a graceful head was that the sort of swan-like neck that goes with it took a bit of coping with when you were especially tired. Lucy chose her pillow with great discrimination. It used to be dear old 'Granny', the Dandidinmont, our other permanent boarder, before she trundled contentedly to her Dog's Paradise. She then accept Jemima on the blissful occasions when that one was so worn out with bouncing that she was actually still for a heavenly half-hour. A human foot would do, but only of the favoured few.

She was the kind of dog for whom it would have been a gross indignity to be dangled on the end of a lead. She had the instinctive good sense to follow you, or to keep you well within view, so that she was at your feet almost before you had opened your mouth to call her.

It was just as well that the lead was not needed, because her rotund, sausage-like proportions did not take too kindly to any sort of harnessing, as I found to my embarrassment when I took her, hooked to the end of a lead, for her first walk.

It was fine while we trotted past the garden hedge as far as the next cottage down the lane. But there...

"Oh horrors," noticed Lucy, "Two great, black giants unpacking a sinister looking monster." - the coal lorry.

"I think I'll go home fast, before they eat me all up..."

And slipping neatly out of her collar, go she did, all four, short legs paddling at Boat Race speed to get her terrified, little self home and dry before the worst could happen.

Puff the Magic Dragon

She was not an enthusiastic hiker at the best of times. Well, would you be if you were three feet long, from nose to tail, and your legs only four inches high? For all her curious shape, though, she was the world's best at sitting up and begging. She did not beg for anything material. None of this unbecoming,

"Gimme a biscuit for my party-trick," lark for Lucy. She sat up that way when she was feeling like a sensible conversation with you and she couldn't reach you conveniently any other way. She would balance for five minutes on end while she held your attention. She could also manage to wag her tail at the same time, if she was so inspired, although she happened to be sitting on it!

They do say that every mother's goose is a swan. Well, Lucy made a most satisfactory swan for me. A funny thing, the other day somebody said,

"You know, you and Lucy were very alike in many ways."

And I truly felt I had received the compliment of the year. One thing we seemed to have in common was our ability to handle dogs. I got a quiet amusement out of watching her when a new dog came in. She took at least a day to sum it up to her satisfaction and, in the meantime, put on an aloof and dis-interested air, when all the time she was giving the matter her deepest consideration.

To be accepted by Lucy after one day was quite an achievement and her judgement was invariably sound.

She was also the only dog wise enough to sum up Katherine and Doug's exuberant Alsatian, Pia, who came to visit at weekends.

Lucy

Pia was large and enormously energetic and, when she came bursting into the sitting-room through the outside door, she did her 'Puff, the Magic Dragon' act most fearsomely! Breathing fire and smoke and roaring defiance to the whole wide world, canine or human, she would leap across the carpet and half the furniture.

Jemima and Toffee would dash for the study with 'ALARM" written all over their faces and most of the dogs in the kitchen would only bark because they felt smugly safe behind the protection of two, closed doors!

But Lucy would appear determinedly from nowhere.

Her round, little body waddling right under dragon-cousin's nose and she would jump on the couch to get a better view of all the fun.

There she stayed, quite still and quiet, but not missing a minute of the enjoyment of it, until the last dregs of excitement were over and the riotous visit had come to its regretful end.

Live hot water bottles

CHAPTER VIII

MOSTLY POODLES

Lucy apart, for the ideal boarder I suppose, as in life itself, one needs the happy medium.

The tiny dogs took up a lot less room but were a frightening responsibility. So small some of them were! The Yorkies, Chuahuas and all the miniatures, lovely as they were, we found we thankfully took fewer and fewer of them as time went by.

Then you come to the other end of the canine scale, the Setters and the Pointers and the like. So huge! And such long necks that, next thing I thought, we should be welcoming giraffes in to board! Moreover, the bigger they were, the more they seemed to want to help.

"Need a hand with the baking?" they gently crooned as they waved an elegant snout over your bowl of pastry or box of eggs. "Or how about letting us peel those carrots for you? Or those new potatoes? Mmm, we do love carrots and potatoes!"

They had only to stand on all fours and their noses were in the bowl or on the plate, or leaning dreamily across the new-baked bread or sniffing hopefully towards the Sunday joint.

So, for kitchen company, we would have had, for choice, the smallsized Labradors and Retrievers, good-tempered Sheep Dogs, non-fighting Cairns and other Terriers, Whippets and Lurchers who keep all four feet on the ground, a long-haired Dachs or two and perhaps a nice mixture of the lot, like Bonnie. No delicate Miniatures, nothing too spoilt, nothing too large... Heavens.! How fussy can you get?

Poodles made good boarders as a rule though the rest of the family were not over enthusiastic over them. Some of them were so small it was rather like cuddling a kitten but they could still jump about ten times as high as themselves. Mostly they gave the impression of being highly nervous, as though they found the world about equal to a ride on the Ghost Train, whereas in fact, the Poodle is extremely hardy, as dogs go, and surprisingly resilient to fate.

Almost invariably her owner introduced her with,

"She has never been away from me before, you know..." and then stood back while I could clearly see all her horrifying, last-minute doubts bolting, like neon signs, through her mind.

What she really meant was that she had just remembered that she took her Poodle up to bed with her every night and never missed her early morning saucer of tea. Suddenly she realised that Topsy was going to have to bed down in the 'Dormitory' while she was at my tender mercies.

I, on the other hand, knew that I had better have dressing gown and slippers handy that night because it was probably going to take more than one bed-time story before the new Poodle was finally convinced that her bedroom was really the best one in the house. It was too. It had the Rayburn cooking away cosily, non-stop all night, while the rest of the house slowly froze to death.

But Poodles are a very easy breed to handle in all other ways. If you talk to them quietly they respond to reasoning most intelligently. Their surface nervousness leads them to try biting, when in doubt, so it does not do to wave your hand in front of their faces without good reason.

One frightened Toy won the rosette for biting before she had crossed the threshold. "Hey", she squeaked as all her fellow-boarders hopefully pranced across the field to give her a rousing welcome.

"The Zoo has come to Town and I am sure they are going to tear me to pieces!"

I lowered a reassuring hand to lift her up to safety,

"What, not that human too, to take me dead or alive? At least I shall go down fighting to the bitter end..." Crunch.. She nearly bit my finger to the bone!

After that she settled down quite nicely but my finger

Cool-snooze time

Elizabeth and the cat-runs

Jenny and Tom

Debbie and Dogs

Honey - Number one lap dog

The 'family' in the field

Elizabeth, Steve and Jemima

Monty - Our Favourite

'My Best Friend'

On the heathrug

We donkeys are special

A family under a pine-tree

'Me and my mate"

Here we are again

Castles everywhere (Herstmonceux)

Wookie - the last of the line

took a rather longer time to feel itself again. Poodles are made of India-rubber inside, they bounce by instinct. But at least it is a light sort of bounce that does not crack the kitchen floor or break the furniture. It is lucky that the Standard Poodles have their feet more firmly on the ground, in all ways. They made very genteel guests although they were big. By our standards, very big, so we did not have many on our books.

One regular customer of long years' standing was a Silver Standard, elegantly named Jupiter, with only three legs on the ground. He lost the fourth in a trap when he was a youngster. Still, since he managed to do a great deal more on his three legs than many dogs can do on four, he was none the worse for it. We could have done with an expanding kitchen when he came though, one bound could take him clear of the hearth-rug and practically into the sink!

It is very often the case with owners of boy Poodles for them to adopt two, rather than only one. Quite often from the same litter. It is good to have two dogs, to be company for each other but, the funny thing is, that it never seems to work amicably for boy Poodles.

At the first break in the business of the day you would almost hear them working up to their first unfriendly engagement.

"Mm, things getting too quiet round here. This won't do at all. I'll just growl my way round Brother Bill over there and stir him up a bit."

He stalks his partner in crime, head down and with his best line in rumbles tuning up inside. The two of them then, one eye cocked to make sure that they were gathering a suitably impressed audience, would then prowl in a tight circle, nose to tail like Sambo's tigers, thinking up all the rudest things imaginable to throw at each other.

"Thought I didn't notice how you were making up to that Corgi last night then? Not that you had any success with her of course. She knows a oneeyed gutter-snipe when she sees one! Grr.. grr!"

"She knows not to condescend to a two bow-legged, flea-bitten rag like yourself, you mean, don't you?"

The growls would get louder.

"Rag, yourself, you mangy old mongrel, you! I'll teach you!" "You cross-eyed son of a hycna, you couldn't teach your grandmother to suck eggs ..."

The air would turn a lurid blue and they were both deliciously on the point of a really bloody onslaught when you would step in and drive the awful pair to their respective corners at opposite ends of the kitchen.

I guess people just can't know that boy Poodles are always jealous of each other.

Another problem that loomed large when boy Poodles were around was, Puddles!

After bouncing and after fighting with each other, it was their favourite occupation, puddling!

Of all the boy Poodles we boarded, and there must have been about twenty altogether, I can only remember four who could be clean. They would even cock their legs as they hurtled through the garden door in an endeavour to get in just one more splash before they anointed the outside world. I had come down in the morning and found a tiny pool beside every conceivable standing obstacle in the kitchen. The thoroughness of it was impressive but, at that early hour, I did not appreciate these finer points.

But the girls are quite different. They usually had particularly charming manners and especially when they came in pairs!

"My dear," chatted Angie in her delightful, broken English. "Allow me to give to ze ears a deleecate lick. How delightful your curls, they set themselves zis morning. And your eyelashes, quite exquiseet!'

"Ah cheri," murmured Rosie languidly, "If only I had your so beautiful feegure. So svelde, so chic, and your shapely legs... yes, do explore right eenside my ears for me, you do it so tastefully."

Their toilette was a mutual topic of endless fascination, quite touching to watch and much more peaceful to the atmosphere in the kitchen.

The two naughtiest boy Poodles in existence however, woefully misnamed Peter and Paul, were an endless source of upheaval and excitement for, apart from their uproarious fights, their one, great aim in life was never to allow themselves to be shut in.

A well-chewed half back door stood witness to that for many years.

They also managed to tear the heavy bolt right off the door into the garden. Hard to credit their teeth and claws with enough strength? But then, we had become very philosophical as to the capabilities of any dog!

Their crowning glory came on the day that I had driven off, through a snowstorm, to do the weeks shopping. Peter and Paul had been battened down in the inside kitchen so that at least there was one extra door between them and freedom. They sat still and quiet only for as long as the sound of the car tyres still crunched on the drive gravel. Then they galvanised into united action.

"Good gracious! Fancy shutting us up in here together!" cried Paul.

"Women," snorted Peter. 'They are all the same. Always wanting to go it all on their own."

"Of course she will need us to help her with her shopping," agreed Paul. "Try eating that door down, There's a good chap."

Chippings and shavings flew this way and that, under their furious attack, but the lock held and Peter bounced frantically around the room to locate another way of escape. He bounced onto the table under the window and landed in the middle of the pile of dog bowls kept there.

They flew in all directions while he manfully tried to eat his way through the framework of each pane of glass.

Paul leapt up beside him.

"Oh, good show! Now we are getting somewhere. Glass? No, that's no use, I've tried breaking that before and I haven't managed it. But this zinc mesh, now..." He shoved it good and hard with his nose and it gave encouragingly.

"Pete, get your teeth into it this side, There's a good fellow, and I will rip this top end down' Rip... rip...tear..bite! The zinc mesh slowly disintegrated under teeth and claws until...

..."There that is just a nice size to squeeze through. Out we go!

Hooray! Free at last! Now we'll show that women who is master in these kennels!"

They pattered happily off to the top of the drive quite oblivious to the snowflakes that drifted over their black, curly coats, their ears, their noses and their happily wagging tails.

"Sniff, sniff... turn right at the gate here, I think, Pete."

"Mm, this is fun. I wonder if we shall catch up with her before she reaches the shops.?"

"Now stop wandering after rabbit smells. We must keep right in the middle of the road, in between the tyre tracks."

"Goodness, what a nice surprise it will be for her to see us!"

The snow was rapidly turning each black Poodle into a shining white figure on four, black, determined legs. Luckily it also slowed down their progress slightly so that I met them, on my return journey, marching, shoulder to shoulder, in the exact centre of the road as I drove round the most dangerous bend in the lane.

The Terrible Twins taking themselves to Market! Neither of them were nonplussed in the slightest.

"Halloo, halloo'" they barked. "We knew how pleased you would be to have us come and look for you. You have not managed all that shopping on your own, without our help, surely?"

"Oh, you have! Well we might as well jump in, then, and make a lovely, snowy mess all over the seats of your car for you."

"Up you go, Paul. My, what a simply, splendid time we are all having!"

"We really are the cleverest Poodles in the world. You know, Pete, I think riding in a car, like this, is even nicer than doing all that walking in the snow. We must do it more often."

I suppose I was lucky that at least they had consented to accept my lift. But suppose that I had been delayed and they had marched out, at the end of the lane, into the middle of the busy London Road? The A275!

In view of their obvious resourcefulness, perhaps they might have hailed a passing taxi and ordered it to help them on their way?

Thinking it over, yes, I rather think they would!

Max

CHAPTER IX

THE DOG THAT DROPPED IN

All round, the sun shone pretty brightly in our kitchen-kennels. Still, there had been times when I could have cheerfully wished some dog a million miles away.

There was the one who splashed down in our swimming pool, for instance. Now, much as we loved our four-footed visitors to feel quite at home during their stay, we did not give them season tickets for the use of our homemade pool. It was enough trouble keeping it clear of the pine-tree's contribution of ten tons of pine-needles a year without that.

In fact, they were rarely invited into the flower-garden at all, except maybe a Pekinese or two. There's favouritism for you!

This one was way above Pekinese proportions since he was an extra heavy, extra ponderous, black Labrador. And he had not yet even registered himself as a client but was just dropping in to look us over.

He dropped in all right!

It was entirely a result of mis-direction. Our layout

of exits and entrances was a bit complicated for the uninitiated as doors and gates were placed in all sorts of strategic positions to suit the human inhabitants as well as the animals. So Dog's Mum happened, in departing from the 'look you over', to veer off through the wrong gate.

Before we all knew it, she, Dog's Dad, myself and the dog, were all congregated, by mistake, in the flower-garden. Here we were being mutually agreeable over our adieus when, "Goodness, what on earth were all the other dogs practically turning somersaults with excitement about on the field side of the netting beyond the pool?" I left Mum and Dad standing and carried out a hasty sortie to check. To reach the fence-netting I had to skirt the swimming pool which was all carefully tucked up for the winter under a Heath-Robinson covering of floating ceiling-tiles stuck to an overall expanse of nylon net.

"Umble, grumble ... splutter, puff," went the ceiling-tiles as I ran past. I stopped in my tracks and saw this long black snout slowly emerging through the whiteness. It looked, for all the world, like an

Our Swimming Pool

enquiring seal coming up for air through the ice of the Arctic wastes!

"Bubble, splash, bubble," it went. Which I took to mean, "Anyone else for a lovely dip?"

"Oh you silly animal," I scolded. "Whatever possessed you to fall in there?" To say I was furious is putting it mildly.

The pool was only three feet deep so I was not too concerned about the dog even if he was catching pneumonia while he was submerged. I was mad about the pool though. .

The ceiling tiles thought it was a new kind of game "How to be an ice floe in three easy lessons." They cracked and broke with tremendous realism while I heaved the culprit out of the murky depths beneath them. I did not dare even think about the new, plastic pool-liner which had cost me over fifty pounds only four months before!

I returned the dripping dog to its owners.

"Dear me," fussed his Mum. "He does look wet! Have you plenty of towels or newspaper to dry him with..? I always use newspaper at home."

"He does love water," said his Dad proudly. "Just can't resist it..."

Miraculously we all survived intact, even the pool, thanks to the acres of foam-sheeting I had bedded the liner onto in the first place. The dog, when he eventually made his debut as a guest, fortunately turned out to be a model of good behaviour and courtesy. He did not even tryout a quick paddle in the kitchen sink!

Instead of deep-sea diving, he took up his stance as fender-in-chief around the Rayburn. He reached just nicely, when spread out lengthways right across the front of it and spent three deliciously cosy weeks living down his fishy reputation and practising instead at being a lovely, good-natured hearth rug.

He was the only dog to have ever tried out our swimming pool for size.

In fact he shared with me the doubtful honour of being one of the only two people to have fallen into it with all their clothes on!

It is not only the lining of our pool that has had its hour of peril. The lining of our kitchen had to withstand almost continuous onslaught.

"Washable wallpaper" it was described as. But not washable after dogs, I think. Through the years it fought a long, and losing, rearguard action against lifted back legs and scratching front ones, with the result that the paper retreated further and further up the wall. Finally it was nearly all hard-gloss paint instead, which was much easier to keep clean anyway.

Since the visitors usually bought their own bedroom furniture we didn't have to be constantly making-do and mending in that direction. As you know, puppies always put a great deal of sound concentration into demolishing their own beds as soon as possible. I did not mind that too much. It is when they practised on someone else's bed that it could prove embarrassing.

Talking of Kittens

Angie and Rosie came in with a dog-size feather- bed to share their slumbers on and I can remember vividly the afternoon when two over-lively Dalmatians had dropped by to spend a night or two. I opened the door, next morning, on a snow scene almost more life-like than the real thing.

Then there was that brand new, and very unusual, collar that our favourite Long-haired Dachshund came in wearing, which mostly disappeared down the throat of another over-busy Dachshund after one industrious night.

It did not seem to do the latter any harm. He loved chewing leather at any time. Though I often wondered what happened to the gold figures it was studded with...

We tried every pet shop in the County to replace it, but in vain. It was a Harrod's special of course, we should have known! After twelve years we were on our fourth hearth rug in front of the Rayburn in the kitchen.

We were on our third arm-chair too.

The new kitten insisted on playing at hide-and-seek in the Springs of it which did not bode too well for that one either.

Talking of kittens... We nearly needed a new cat altogether, once, after two dogs had purposely mistaken our newly-resident Tom kitten for a Christmas cracker!

It was this way.

Long-haired Dachs. again, but black ones this time, and as full of ideas as a wagon-load of chimpanzees. They had already spent their fortnight with us giving the fence-netting their individual attention, with very satisfactory results from their point of view.

Considering how many times they had penetrated into the garden under, through and round every minutest weakness in the wire-mesh, it is surprising they had not collided with Tom kitten in the wide open spaces before. Perhaps they had, without us knowing it, and Tom had given them back so much cheek that they had sworn to get their revenge at all costs.

Their stay was almost over. In fact, I was ushering them out of the kitchen and across the hall and into the sitting-room where their Mama was all ready to resume ownership. Then they caught sight of Tom-kitten sitting on the divan in the hall and, for once, minding his own business.

"Do you see what I see?" yelled Banger.

"You bet I do," shouted back Chips.

With an even louder "Tally Ho" and "Forward the Buffs", they both leapt into the Chase.

"Shiver my whiskers," spluttered Tom, "Time to make myself scarce, I think"

He headed for the pear-tree in the middle of the lawn, out of the open front door at top speed. But Banger and Chips had got into fourth gear before Tom had even had time to start his engine properly. And then there was his tail... that was nearly a foot behind him, as usual, and just within reach of Chips' nose as they flashed past the garden seat.

"Gotcher", he grunted. "Here, catch, Banger."

His partner in crime sunk his own sharp teeth into the soft fur behind Tom's head and then they both pulled!

Tom's language was blue, black, and more than eloquent and you could hardly blame him. With a pair of vices tugging at him from both ends at once, he was feeling more like a Christmas cracker every minute.

Before the Big Bang, Elizabeth and Jenny had raced across to the rescue. But it had been a near thing. Tom sat at the top of the pear-tree to watch their car drive away. He was still swearing the rudest things he could think of, under his breath. He counted up his nine lives carefully, on both paws. Then he counted them again.

"Oh bother, there's another one gone!" he said.

Not all the boarders were so energetic fortunately. In

fact, practically every dog over the age of about ten, came complete with his neat packet of the tiniest heart-pills imaginable. We were getting as good as the dentist at saying, "Open wide, please," and popping them in twice a day.

Quite a few even had diabetes or liver trouble or some other chronic ailment it (and its owner) had learned to live with. One veteran Poodle, on a special diet for life, used to move in complete with a huge supply of deep-frozen tripe which monopolised the entire freezer compartment of our fridge for all of the first three-quarters of his stay.

For all the draw-backs to dog-boarding, however, the feeding, the cleaning, the commotion and the responsibility, there was one permanent advantage in living in our glorified dog-kennel: You did have to be careful to shut doors and windows to stop the inmates from getting out... but you didn't have to give a thought to stopping the uninvited humans from getting in!

He may not be as neat and tidy (and certainly he is not so unobtrusive) as a Chubb lock, but a madly barking dog, behind the flimsiest pane of glass, is enough to keep out the most determined burglar. They are probably shouting,

"Oh do come in! We are so pleased to see you."

"Have you come for lunch or would you rather share this extra chewed bit of bone with me?" "I say, you have livened up our afternoon. You should have come yesterday. The old dragon was out for hours then and we could have shown you all over the house from top to bottom."

But the would-be burglar can't afford to risk it and the noise (welcoming or otherwise) upsets his Trade Union rules of, 'Quiet is essential at all times'. We found all this out quite by accident in our very first full season.

Keith came home from work on the Monday, "Our next-door neighbours had a break-in on Saturday. Lost all their silver and all their brass."

"Ooh", All the children were thrilled and frightened all at the same time. "We wish we had seen him".

Next-door is three acres away, so it is not surprising that they didn't. But there was more to come.

"And up the road, the new people were broken into as well".

That made it more alarming. The children looked at each other apprehensively, "

He must have gone past our house! I wonder why he did not burgle us?"

"That's easy," I laughed (a little shakily, I must confess). We have nothing remotely worth stealing."

"Oh Mum," protested Elizabeth. "There is my long-haired Guinea-pig!

"And my collection of Beatles records," put in Katherine.

"Yes, and about half-a-crown's worth of gold in Tinker's fur," laughed Keith.

Jenny had been absorbing the news silently in the background. When the excitement had died down she sidled hopefully over to me.

"I tell you what, Mum, I can easily stay at home from school and look after everything whenever you want to go off shopping," she offered, earnestly...

The break-ins went on for quite a time, especially into the larger houses that stood on their own. Some of them did have one dog, or even two, on guard. None of them, however, had ten... or eleven...

The piece-de-resistance came about three months later when a smart, black police-car oozed to a halt outside our gate.

Out jumped two marvellously young and handsome detectives and strode down our drive to the door.

"We have a man here," they told us, "Who states that he broke in to this house on the sixteenth of August last." Broken in! Us!

They were so positive, I almost believed them. Then I did a rapid bit of thinking. August! I brought out the Dog-diary that sits by the telephone.

"No," I said finally, "He must be mistaken. You see, on that day in August, this year, we were boarding thirteen dogs!'"

The C.I.D. were respectful and even a little

impressed. They explained further, "We are driving this chap round and he is pointing out all the houses he thinks he burgled this summer."

"Well, perhaps he has muddled us up with someone else, do you think? There is another white house just along the road, only it is tidier," I explained. They were so nice. We did enjoy their visit!

Later the phone rang and it was our dashing cavaliers on the other end. "Yes Madam," came the verdict. "You were quite right. Our man now says he did not break into your house after all. In fact," he concluded, "Yours was the only house in the whole neighbourhood that he does not seem to have had a go at..." And so it remained, I am glad to say!

I am not sure that the rest of the family were quite so whole-heartedly with me there..

Keith, for one, was so good at digging holes for burglar traps. It was a shame such a talent was uncalled for. He kept his hand in by a subterranean inspection of the drainage every now and then but, I could see, the results were not nearly so sensational.

Katherine and I were truly sorry that we could offer no more opportunities for visits from our heart throbbing detectives. My, they were delicious!

Elizabeth did not mind a bit. She put her Guinea-pig under lock and key in a cat-run and moved Hammy up to her bedroom. Then all precautions taken, she promptly put the whole thing out of her head. She had just heard of a lovely white rabbit that she might be able to get for us, and free!

Jenny just trooped philosophically back to school. Oh well, it would soon be the Christmas holidays and it might even snow! She cuddled Conker absent-mindedly and he gave her a consoling face-wash of licks. As Burglar-Alarm-in-chief he came off quite the best, carte-blanche to be as rude and uproarious as he liked to everyone who knocked on the door - just in case!

And a lovely excuse for stirring up the Whole household to a deafening chorus of barks and yaps every time he thought he heard the tiniest unidentifiable, noise!

How to be an ice flow in three easy lessons

CHAPTER X

CATS' CRADLES

After six whole chapters full of almost nothing but their antics, you must think our lives were devoted exclusively to dogs. The dogs would have liked to think so, too. But then, what dog doesn't truly believe it is the only animal in the world worth having?

So, before they all become even more full of their own importance, let us leave them blissfully asleep on the back step and tiptoe round to the garden to meet our other boarders, the cats.

I have a great respect for cats. The independence of them and the courage. We women inveigh against the unkind fate that has thrust us, willy nilly, into a man's world, but think what sort of a place it must seem to a cat!

Kitty - a wash that is

Menaced by dogs outside every garden fence, Menaced even by their own species, and that often inside the garden fence as well. Also, often expected to hunt for at least half their food and competing, in the country here at least, with foxes, owls, rats and even hedgehogs that may lurk in any shadow of their trail.

Ninety-percent of the world is against them but they still sit serenely in the porch cleaning every speck of their impeccable fur with the minutest attention to detail and only pause to survey the world at large with that aristocratic urbanity that only a cat can perfect.

Second only to watching the miniature, lightning movements of the hamster attending to his bath-time ritual, is the pleasure I take in sitting, in relaxed silence, to watch any cat washing herself. She is soft and graceful for all her intentness. A swan does not more elegantly incline its neck. While the obliging pink tongue charges each delicately proffered paw, in turn, with endless cleaning material.

And very potent washing powder it must be too, in the way it produces a wash 'whiter than white' in effortless supply...

It is the utter peacefulness of the whole operation that delights so much. Calm and deliberate, and in some magic way, as I watch, I find that all the tight knots inside me suddenly work themselves loose. My shoulders begin to sag comfortably and for a heavenly oasis of time I sit and learn anew the potential calm and serenity of life.

How different from a dog! There we would be, sitting round the kitchen table at lunch, when all of a sudden the most revolting, scrunching, slobbering, sucking sound fills the room. I look round, frowning severely on the long suffering family:

"For goodness sake, MUST you make that awful noise when you eat?" But I would be met, on all sides, with puzzled innocence and the noise would continue unabashed...

...Yes, just one of the dogs inspired to carry out cleaning operations on a couple of square inches of its fur, under the table, with a noise like mealtime in the pig-house!

And indeed, one of the very first impressions you get from a close-ish acquaintanceship with dogs is their cheerful lack of refinement over the most delicate aspects of life!

They sniff with enormous enjoyment at everything and everybody, and the nastier the smell, the more abandoned the gusto. They may casually poke a welcoming nose into the face of a new arrival but they make no bones about which end they really prefer investigating - and it definitely isn't the front end!

The cats, admittedly, were in separate runs when they came in to board, so they were a bit handicapped in showing off the worst side of their natures. For all their outward poise they were highly suspicious of everyone and everything. But not for nothing are a cat's eyes slanted, and there is a considerable amount of oriental 'face' to be reckoned with when meeting strangers.

Very seldom did any cat give his paw in friendship to the occupant of the next-door run. But we found that one very good way to wheedle a pussycat into letting down his hair was to pop Elizabeth's Guinea-pig into the run next door.

We often used to let Guinea take over a vacant run out of season, especially when the grass needed a good cut. Elizabeth was quite right, after all, when she had tried to talk us into substituting a guinea-pig for a pair of shears! What is more he actually enjoyed the grass-cutting, which is more than I did.

Cats and more cats

But nearly as much as grass, Guinea loved company, and he had no inhibitions whatsoever of race of creed. He just liked sitting down to a right old gossip.. chatter, chatter, chatter,.. He was pretty undemanding of his acquaintances and was happy to monopolise the conversation if that is the way you wanted it.

He clambered up against the dividing wire-netting in obvious delight at the advent of the newcomer: "So pleased to meet you," he prattled happily, "And what do you think of the runs, then? Not too bad, are they? Do pop round to this one whenever you feel like it." His little white nose poked invitingly through the mesh and puss would give an off-hand sniff.

Guinea paused for breath. ..what he would obviously dearly love to have done was to scoot round and stand on the door-step next door complete with a tray of tea and biscuits, like the neighbour who knocks you up even before the removal-men have finished unloading.

"There, have a cup of tea, dearie and you'll feel a treat you will... Lovely place you've got here... Ever so nice to have you next door.." His little furry tum would bulge with importance and his whiskers wiggle with welcome.

The cat would sit down and give Guinea enough attention to make him feel it was all well worth while. It did not take much to please the little chap. So he would hop off back to his shelter to have a good wash and brush up, muttering to himself,

"Nice chap that. Good class, too, I shouldn't wonder. Friendly though, likes a bit of at chat over the fence and you can't ask for more than that, can you? Better give my nose an extra brush over where he blew on it though. My, oh my! What at busy life this is!"

The cat, not to be outdone, would preen herself with measured indifference. However, you noticed that whereas last night she prowled around the run very suspiciously and noisily, to night she beds down at 'lights out' without any trouble and sleeps, peacefully curled up, until break- fast time.

I once read that only someone who was devoted to cats would be mad enough to think of boarding them. For the monetary rewards are low and the work and outlay are, respectively, hard and high. At the time I frankly disbelieved it. After so many years on the job now I go with it, wholeheartedly, all the way.

To start with, when we had our six runs built, they cost nearly a hundred pounds without counting the inside 'furniture' of timber sleeping-houses, baskets, cat-litter trays and paving. Nor did it include the plastic proofing to keep six-feet of each twelve-foot run dry, or the sheeting and rustic fencing which were needed for extra protection along the sides.

The surrounding wire-netting had to be expensive, half-inch mesh. The fineness of it was not to keep the cats from getting out because a larger mesh would have done that just as well and a lot more cheaply. It was to stop the birds getting in! You would quickly have seen the point of that when you had stood and watched a sleek Siamese, with pricked ears and swishing tail, sitting thirsting for the blood of a saucy sparrow showering him with raindrops from not six-feet above his head.

It did not stop the mice from trying their luck. I don't know whether some of the mouse clan became more inquisitive than the rest or perhaps they played mouse version of, 'Last Across the Road'.

But on rare occasions the pathetic remains of their sad error of judgement, mousewise, could be seen in the morning inside the run.

I have seen cats (and dogs too, for that matter) kennelled in a sort of rabbit hutch contraption where they are forced to sit patiently day after day eking out the weary hours, staring or sleeping, until their longed-for release. To be perfectly fair, many years ago I can remember leaving our own cat in such quarters without a qualm... and she seemed none the worse for it either.

But standards of humane-ness have risen balloon-like, like the standards of living I suppose. Ideally now each run needs to be a good three feet wide and twelve-feet long for the cats' comfort, and over six-feet high for YOUR comfort. I know that, ours were mostly under six-feet and gave me back-ache every feeding-time and an extra bonus of a cracked skull whenever the doorway succeeded in catching me in an unwary off-day.

The groundwork can be lots of things from solid concrete to bare earth. The cats prefer it nice soft grass, but the Health People plump for good, hard cement. They don't have to foot the bill of course, but it is obviously much easier to keep clean.

With feline stars in my eyes I happily grassed each cat-run, to begin with, and carefully dug a garden for each. I spread catmint for their enjoyment and bedded down a large log for claw-sharpening. I even planted marigolds and nasturtiums for OUR enjoyment.!

I guess the cats sized up my flower gardens as a sort of Ritz-type loo and a few weeks of their industrious scratching soon reducing my airy-fairy notions to a much more practical level. But the grass remained, and it was a satisfying sight, in that corner of the garden, to see those elegant stretches of warm fur luxuriously sunning themselves, on summer mornings in peaceful and utter contentment.

When we were siting the runs, it seemed good thinking to study the likes and dislikes of our own cat on the subject, which she considered a sheltered aspect and which time of day she welcomed the sun and which the shade. That was interesting in itself, for I hadn't realised before that she never sought the afternoon sun. Apparently noon-time was cool-snooze time and she curled up, from choice, in the shade of the north-facing barns.

It made sense however, so we obligingly sited the runs roughly north-east to south-west so that they could drink in the morning sun but shelter from the heavy afternoon heat under the spreading branches of the pine-tree.

Doesn't it sound delicious?

The pine-tree thought so too and oozed quarts of sticky resin out of his old sides they were shaking with laughter at such a huge joke...

We had never had a large pine-tree in our garden before. You don't see them all that often - and no wonder!

The first thing I knew about it was when I trotted round the runs, in late summer, and wondered why my hair kept getting caught on the roof-netting. Then I looked up and found myself gazing into a massed attack of needle pointed arrows.

Ah well, if you invade Sussex I guess you must expect the SaxonHastings treatment! That's obviously what our pine-tree thought too, for we fought our battle every year, 'The Battle of The Pine-needles'. They rained down in their thousands and covered cat-runs, patio, flowers and grass in unbiased generosity... and during all those years, I still found no way of removing them from a hundred and twenty square-feet of netting than by pulling them through, painstakingly, by hand, and it was about as comfortable as picking gooseberries!

Only one point did I score in the tussle. But I am rather proud of even that small victory. That was when I dreamed up the idea of gathering pile upon pile of needles off the autumn lawn and spreading them triumphantly all along the muddy path that the dogs used to wander out to their field. A three-inch deep layer of pine-needles makes a wonderful paving and it's heaps cheaper than concrete!

So the cat-runs were sited just so! Each was furnished with its small house of wood, complete with a large, plastic window. Well, what cat doesn't love looking down its nose out of the window? The doorways were curtained off to form an economical cat-flap, the earth trays were obligingly provided for the 'necessary' and the first visitors settled down for the night.

No, that's wrong.

We settled down for the night. The visitors unwound their warm bodies from their cosy beds, stretched each paw tentatively for action, poked a wary nose through the curtain and, in a flash, were transformed into one penetrating L.P. of yeowels!

It wouldn't have been quite so painful if their runs had been, say, down the bottom of the paddock or behind the barns. But no, in our dreaming innocence, we had gone and sited them just a robin's hop outside the two main bedroom windows!

Now noise, as we of the modem age know only too well, is just about the most intruding, infuriating, impossible sort of thing to keep out. You shut your window and it comes down the chimney. You block your ears up tight, but it still gets in. You worm right down under the bed-clothes (where you nearly die of suffocation) and you can still hear it. We couldn't even throw a boot at the offenders, in the time-honoured tradition; we had made them invulnerable behind their chain-mail defences...

Give them their due, it was not every cat that serenaded the moon. Some of them saved it up for welcoming the dawn! 4a.m., we discovered in mid-summer! But which ever end of the night they performed at best, by the end of the first week it was unanimous that "Something must be DONE."

The first kitten who came in

So the night-runners were, alas, deprived of their choral freedom and a large board was fixed in front of each cat-house until morning. Even then, the holes some of them managed to squeeze through! They would have given a large mouse quite a bit of negotiating and it was "no holds barred" when it came to tearing the carefully tailored plastic windows or shredding up the drape of gay curtaining.

The odd thing was that the cats who came in during that first season sported the loudest miaows and most persistent repertoires of all the cats we ever had since. But even so, you can well understand that our favourite cat of all was the snow-white Persian picture-puss who had never learned to talk at all...

Kittens were the most fun of all, of course. In fact, the first infant who came to stay came up to bed with me every night because I was sure he would feel lonely all by himself in a big run. Even the wild kittens had purrs twice as big as themselves as soon as they had settled down. The tame kittens never even waited for an

Tom, the unconcerned!

introduction before they turned on their loud and unreserved approval of us, the runs and the whole delightful new world they had just discovered.

Tinker on the other hand, gave the runs a very wide berth, especially if there was a Siamese swearing away at a neighbour to assert its oriental superiority. But the cat she disliked most of all was the one that came to stay. You have met him in passing already. Tom Kitten he was called and a more life-like edition of naughty Tom Kitten would have been hard to find. He stole the butter out of the dish and the milk out of the jug, the food out of the dog's bowls - and everybody's heart!

He arrived as a starving stray and was really only staying the night or two en route for the local animal rescue centre. But somehow the day of departure kept getting put off and, in the meantime, Tom's purrs kept getting louder and louder... He used to -purr so loudly I think he even frightened himself at times. and he was the prettiest softest grey you ever saw.

So in the end he succeeded in brain-washing us into thinking that a new, soft, grey kitten cat was just what we really needed.

"All right, he can stay...if he doesn't mind the dogs."

Tinker had always avoided them like the plague and kept carefully to her part of the house. Doesn't mind dogs! Tom stalked into the kitchen as though he had been born and bred at Crufts - or the Battersea Dogs' home.'

"Right then, where are all these dogs?"

The first one advanced curiously and Tom gave him

such a dirty look that he suddenly remembered a very pressing appointment outside!

The second one thought we had sportingly provided him with a toy rabbit and bounced up all eager and hopeful. But Tom just didn't seem to get the idea at all and retaliated by taking a hefty swipe at the waving tail and the dog retreated into a quiet corner with a baffled expression on his face.

Tom sat where he was, in the middle of the kitchen floor and in the middle of the remaining handful of boarders, and unconcernedly gave himself a concentrated overhaul. Next to thieving, washing was his favourite occupation. Then he made a careful survey of each dog-bed in turn, the baskets, the boxes, the rugs and the pillows (there was always an interesting selection) and when he had pinpointed the most inviting he just stepped in, curled up and went fast asleep...

It was a great performance and established his supremacy in the kitchen for good and all.

Actually he preferred the dogs' fur to the dogs' bedding. On winter days, when as many dogs as possible were sprawled in a sleeping heap on the rug in front of the Rayburn, he would wait, impassively, until all were comfortably arranged, and then he would descend quietly, but purposefully, and ooze himself into a small nest which would somehow materialise itself right in the middle of them all. There he would stay, curled up tight and fast asleep and surrounded by his deliciously warm, accommodating, live hotwater bottles.

Mind you, sometimes he would take things almost too far and, more than once, I have been dragged out of my own nice warm bed by the banshee howling of a dog about six times Tom's size and come storming into the kitchen to find the dog sitting helplessly, and loudly protesting, on the floor by its own bed - in which young Tom would be curled up, his paws happily tight over his ears, snoring his head off...

I suppose it was too much to hope he would get on well with cats as well as with dogs. The short answer was.. that he didn't. Tinker was terrorised into every corner of her existence.

We allowed her the undisputed refuge of the sitting-room and she used to bolt into it as though all the devils in hell were on her tail. Or we would look up from peacefully stroking her before the sitting-room fire to see Tom's livid face glaring through the window, his ears flattened in hate and his eyes tawny with fury.

He used to crouch in wait for her behind the bushes in the garden and chase her mercilessly over the hills and far away to a blood-curdling chorus of yells and squeals.

It was just as well he didn't achieve such an impressive result when he sauced the pony in the same way. For His Naughtiness used to lie in ambush whenever he spotted the pony and the donkey being led through the garden on their way to bed and, just as the trampling hooves were nearly upon him, he would spring out, like a small, grey dervish, and turn a somersault of high glee to see the two of them snort and start back in surprise.

ˈBut one day he heard the call of the Wild too strongly. In the magic way with cats, one minute he was sitting, lording it, on the kitchen table and the next moment he had disappeared... and we never saw him again.

We did get a postscript of news of him, though. Mrs. Thomas, up at the farm, in Cooksbridge, said there was a small, grey cat in residence, all of a sudden, up in the big barn. She knew it must be Tom - he was so naughty!

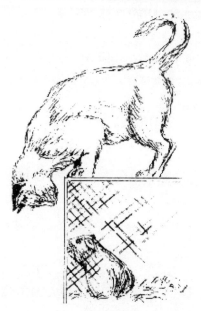

Pleased to meet you

CHAPTER XI

BUTTERCUPS AND DONKEYS

Thank you, Tom, you have led us nicely on to the next arrivals to come on board our Ark and join the family.

It was inevitable, in Sussex, that a donkey should amble its way in at our garden gate sooner or later. If you drive through our countryside on a sunny summer's day, you might be forgiven for drawing the obvious conclusion that, along with the wheat, the barley and the potatoes, we also broadcast a good sprinkling of donkey-seed over our fields each winter. For there are donkeys everywhere!

We had four up our lane, for a start.

Then there were the Donkey Studs, the Donkey Clubs, the Donkey Derbys and the Donkey Shows. Soon they'll be having a corner all to themselves on the County Badge along with those elusive martlets!

It is the clay that is at the bottom of it. It grows grass like other soils grow corn and vegetables. Long, luscious grass that grows all day and all night, all summer and most of the winter too, and donkeys eat grass like anything!

When I had ordered, 'At least an acre of ground,' from those longsuffering House-agents, I hadn't dreamed it could consist of a long-haired turf on top of soil that would be like uncooked treacle-cake all winter, toughening up to solid, stale rock-buns in the summer.

Sussex clay.

So there we were now, a small, struggling clan of very average gardeners, with a quarter of an acre of tangled mass, politely called the vegetable garden, a fair stretch of semi-civilised lawn and beds one could reasonably take for the flower-garden and nearly half an acre of grazing now netted-in for a dog's paradise.' And still the grass went on growing...

I kept losing the tiny dogs in the longest patches out in their field and it was agonising trying to wade through the nettles and thistles to keep a check on the boundary netting. The morning that even Jupiter, the three-legged Standard Poodle found a hole large enough to let himself through onto the road (and back, fortunately) I was finally jolted into crying determinedly that,

"Something must be done."

It wasn't even just the paddock grass either. Goading us into desperation, on the other side of the drive, was the vegetable garden which waved itself higher and higher with grass and giant-size buttercups every year.

Keith, as digger-in-chief, almost had it half-tamed

when he was sent off on an endless succession of missions abroad to solve the World's oil pollution problems. His mantle fell on old Sam Drew from the village who cycled up to 'do' for the vegetable-garden every Friday.

We all enjoyed his visits immensely.

"Them buddercups," he would rumble darkly as he stomped doggedly in for elevenses with yet another spade broken.

"Them buddercups do own that bit of garden I'm thinking. But I'll do for them yet!" Honours considered even by this valiant declaration of purpose, he would then sit down to strengthen his arm with hot tea and buttered buns.

It was the cue Conker had been waiting for since breakfast. Sam probably knew really that he was fighting a losing battle with 'them buddercups', so maybe this encouraged him to try out his skill on our puppy instead. After the first bun had disappeared, along with two cups of tea, down his own throat, he would give the matter his undivided attention.

A donkey on the lawn

"Sit,... Speak for it... .Now. . !"

Puppy was only too happy to oblige for fresh, buttered buns. He was a very quick learner where food was concerned, and they got through buns, biscuits, tea and endless lumps of sugar to their mutual satisfaction with unfailing regularity.

..Then they would resume The Battle of the Buttercups..

But eventually even Sam (and Conker) gave up the unequal struggle. The vegetable-garden exchanged knowing winks with the over-grown dogfield and probably craftily threw in a few sackfuls of buttercup-seed to celebrate. They gave a very perfunctory glance at the little horse-box when it arrived at the gate with its long-eared occupant.

"Not another addition to the menagerie," sighed the field, languidly. "Perhaps I had better spread that far corner with a double helping of nettle roots after all."

"Oh, I shouldn't worry," said the vegetable-garden as he nudged up another fine crop of ground-elder, "Whatever it is, it will never be a match for the likes of us!"

That's what they thought!

Strangely enough it was the visit of a former neighbour, from concrete Suburbia, that actually set us on our donkey-path. She happened along on that fateful afternoon when Jupiter, the Standard Poodle had hopped his three-legged way out of the field through a nettle-hidden hole (and in again, luckily). She was met by my barrage of fury.

I can hear her quiet voice now as she mildly commented, "You ought to get a donkey, you know"

"A donkey! Heavens! We have enough dogs and cats and guinea pigs and hamsters.."

She withstood the deluge and patiently persisted,

"No, I don't mean just as a pet. I mean as a grass-cutter." Just at that moment, who should breeze in from school, but Elizabeth.

That settled it!

The grass in our field may have grown but the grass under Elizabeth's busy feet never has the slightest chance.

The next day was Saturday and by early afternoon I found myself diffidently pushing open the office-door at Cherry Tree Farm.

Cherry Tree Farm, which is a horse and donkey sanctuary outside East Grinstead, lives up to its lovely name in every respect. A picture-book cottage suns itself happily in the arms of the sort of garden you only see on country calendars and all around are apple-pie clean stables and enclosures full of peaceful, contented horses and donkeys.

It is a haven of kindness and hospitality and not a bit worried that, across the road, the awe-inspiring Tower of Babel, in the form of the Mormon Tabernacle, looms over it in such a very superior way.

Which reminds me of the legend of the first donkey. Perhaps you remember it too?

The first four guardian angels were furious!

"Everything is going wrong," they said before the Almighty's throne.

"There's Eve led astray and then Adam," grumbled the first.

"And now Cain has put paid to Abel," scolded the second. "Its no good inventing a creature as clever as Man, and giving him the World to play with, if you don't teach him how to behave."

The Almighty stroked His beard thoughtfully as He pondered the problem. With his other hand he gently tickled his pet donkey pensively behind the ears.

"If they only had something as kind and as sensible as you, my donkey," he said,

"Then perhaps they would learn to live together and love each other as we do." He looked wistfully at his favourite pet.

The donkey slowly raised his head.

"I'll go," he said. "I know it will be hard. They'll beat me, laugh at me, say I am a fool. But for you, Master, I will always be gentle, kind and lowly. For you I will teach them how to carry their burdens uncomplainingly, to go with peace and patience through the world, to serve and follow and obey."

"That's my brave Donkey," said the Lord. "And so that all men shall know you come from Me, I shall seal my mark upon you." With his finger he drew a big cross over the donkey's shoulders.

The donkey looked sadly round at the green pastures of his Heavenly home and, lastly, into the compassionate eyes of his Heavenly Master.

"Give me a voice that I may call you when I am feeling just a little homesick," he begged. "And make it loud, so that it will reach you, and like no other creature's voice so that you will always recognise it straight away and know that it is I who calls".

And that is how the donkey came to serve Mankind. And that is why his bray is indeed the most ear-shattering and unearthly noise you have ever heard.

However, back to my story.

"We would like a donkey, please." But even Elizabeth's magic could not bring us instant success. Other people, it appeared, also wanted donkeys and in fact there was a long waiting list of would-be donkey owners.

"We have two fields" we volunteered.

"All our donkeys have to be stabled as well," they patiently countered.

"Yes, we have two stables.."

"..and dogs to keep him company," was Elizabeth's further inducement. Perhaps it was Elizabeth after all who brought us luck again, or maybe - just maybe - Mr. Gibbs suddenly remembered their favourite, homeborn foal, Ringo, who was becoming just the tiniest bit of a problem! He was full-grown all of a sudden and raring to transfer himself from their picture book garden to someone else's overgrown acres.

"A young one? Oh, yes please."

"All right then. We can let you have young Ringo. We'll send our Inspector to you first to arrange everything."

Another Inspector! We felt we were beginning to collect them like milk-bottle tops. Still, they always turned out such nice men...

"Do go and talk to the donkeys if you like. They are over there by the far gate."

We happily trotted off, secretly hoping we would recognise them when we saw them since, awful to confess, at that time we scarcely knew one end of a donkey from the other.

They gave us a lovely welcome. Their long ears were pricked up as though the whisper had gone round already that we had come to adopt one of them and their long, velvety noses hovered encouragingly over the gate to give us friendly snuffles.

We advanced naively and I was promptly bitten by the largest, who turned out to be our destined pet.

It was an appropriate introduction. Ringo obviously hadn't been told the legend of the First Donkey, and we all had a lot to learn, especially me!

The children were at school and I and Conker provided the welcoming committee, all on our own, when the horse-box arrived. Ringo walked amiably out and we installed him in his new stable to rest from the journey. "Pop him into the field after an hour or so," the kindly manager advised.

Just as well he stipulated that long, for it took me all that time and a bit more, to work out the intricacies of fixing our new halter around our new donkey's neck!

I tried it this way up. I tried it that way up. Even the donkey began to look puzzled. So in the end, Conker and I took the halter into the kitchen with us. With the 'book of words', thank heavens for the library again, propped up in front of us on the table, I finally managed to fix it quite respectably round the neck of one mystified mongrel before transferring it gingerly, but successfully, to the neck of its rightful wearer.

After that, the hundred yard journey out to the field seemed almost uneventful and the dog and I retired to have a much needed rest before the family hurtled home to 'tea and donkey'.

For two very enjoyable days we were all the proud owners of an enchanting and model donkey... Then we looked out of the window on the Saturday morning and there, most mysteriously, was our too enchanting donkey now miraculously transported into our neighbour's adjoining field.

There he stood, innocently nibbling the grass, not an ear twitching to show how it had been done.

"He couldn't have jumped the gate. After all he's only a donkey, silly." But the first tiny seed of doubt was sown and, next day, he grew carelessly indiscreet and took a flying leap, like a Grand National champion, this time when somebody was looking.

'Donk'

After that, whenever he and Conker were resting from chasing each other round and round the field, Ringo's blissful occupation was to work out new ways of appearing on the wrong side of whatever fence or barrier restricted him.

When his Houdini powers were at their height, I spent practically all my spare time darting into the Study to check, through the window, that our lawn was not sprouting an errant donkey, and the family war-cry became,

"Close the front-door, someone, quick.."

For if Ringo was first in the race - and he was still working to Aintree standards - he would be inside, and enjoying all the home-comforts of the sitting-room hearthrug, with enormous gusto!

We bought fifty-feet of strong rope, thinking a truce might be called by tethering. But this was peanuts to a resourceful donkey. He just went on walking round and round the nearest tree until he lay at the foot of it, so firmly trussed, that we had to rush out and saw through our 'good strong rope' with the carving knife to set him free.

So much for the, "your donkey will enjoy being tethered on a juicy patch," claim. That was in another book our donkey had not yet read.

Mind you, when I returned from shopping mornings in Lewes, and he was still in his field, I was secretly more charmed than I would admit by the welcoming brays that rang round the countryside.

"Aarrh," old Henry would say, in the house up on the hill, "There goes Mrs. Fleming's Arse again!" And Mrs. Fleming's 'arse' he ever was.

However the original intent of procuring a do it yourself grass-cutter was amply justified. But, along with the grass, we lost twelve flourishing laurel bushes, five good, new, apple trees, nine silver birches and two gum trees. Two rhododendron's and one weeping willow were removed, at stump level, but actually survived.

Then we lost the first wall!

It lay between the area outside the kitchen-door that the dogs cross to get to their field and the open stable that the donkeys use when they are in the 'vegetable-garden'. (We were boarding an extra donkey by then). It was a pretty little brick wall with a gate leading through the centre of it.

The dogs were always very fond of this wall on their side of it. It was fabulous as an incentive to a try-out cock-of-the-leg for the boys. While the girls, my Lucy especially, used to use it as an old-type solar-reflecting system as it caught the sun full face most of the day.

"Caught," you'll notice I say. Not, "Catches." Ominous, isn't it?'

It was just unfortunate that it was in this barn that the donkeys were stabled all that winter and fortuitously too that the straw, that winter, was full of lice so there were the donkeys with coats that itched and tickled like anything and here was this nice, nobbly, old wall just outside their barn and so convenient for their scratching-post....

They scratched and rubbed to their hearts' content until the fateful afternoon when Jenny tossed a casual remark over the top of it at me, who had just let the dogs out in full spate after their lunch.

"This bit of wall is getting quite wobbly, Mum. Look!"

In my horrified ears all the trumpets of Jericho sounded as the entire wall thereupon came, slowly but ever so remorselessly, crashing down at my feet.

Don't tell me now that miracles don't ever happen. For Somebody, and it certainly wasn't me or Jenny, who were both rooted to the spot in horror, shooed every dog out of the thirty square-feet that the wall flattened within a matter of split seconds! Not a paw was brushed, not a whisker tickled.

We never rebuilt the wall. We replaced it with a high fence of wood reinforced with deeply-sunk, oak pillars. But you should have seen the super door-step we suddenly had. It was made of solid brick and it was the split~ image of that wall that the donkeys tumbled down all those years ago!

Then we lost our first fence!

This time Ringo was in the dogs' paddock pretending to be the perfect roto-scythe.

We were busy in the garden, engrossed in adding to the cat-runs, when suddenly there was a rending sound off-stage...He just hadn't been able to contain himself any longer, so he had put his strong shoulder under the lower fencing rail and heaved it straight up out of the ground, netting and all, and was now coming at us full pelt like a marauding elephant!

Eventually when every fence, every hedge and every gate had proved its failure, ten times over, to confine our neat-footed pet, we rang the Sanctuary in desperation.

To the music of determined blows not only on the door of the main stable, but on the tough old frame of the door as well, I appealed,

"We love him but... I think perhaps one a little quieter (a lot less versatile, I meant). Yes, I think he must be bored and needs some company." When what I really meant was, "If he gets out of that stable and teaches himself to drive our car, there'll be no holding him this side of King's Cross!"

The manager, however, was kindness itself. But there, I should have learned by now that donkey-people almost invariably are.

And so 'Mrs. Fleming's arse' was replaced by the quietest, gentlest, most delightfully behaved donkey that ever twitched an ear.

Yet, looking back in thoughtfulness and wonder at how it did happen, as happen it did, that our problem child, who had in his time so rudely butted the Rector half around the field, one breath-taking day behaved with all the docility, the courtesy and the fore-bearance of his wisest grandsires?

Did he remember that favourite bed-time story that his mother rocked him to sleep with when he was just a foal? Or did the dark cross on his fur suddenly seem to weigh upon him?

For on Palm Sunday he trotted the long mile to the village as surely as his ancestor had picked her dainty way up the rough trail to the golden gates of Jerusalem, and for a long hour he willingly lent his back to an unending line of small Sunday-school children all clamouring,

"My turn! My turn!"

Donk and his youngest stable boy

They warmed their hands in his soft, grey fur. They stroked his long ears and they shouted enough to send him jumping every fence in sight. But for his brief hour of glory he was a donkey transformed.

He trotted - carefully, responsible of his precious burdens. He stood with angelic patience while they scrambled on and off him excitedly. And surely his furry ancestors looked down on him with great pride, softly breathing down their velvet noses,

"Well done, little donkey! Well done!"

Our second donkey may have had a name when he was being beaten and kicked by the owner of his youth. When we first had him, he would cringe back even when you lifted your hand up to stroke him and he was terrified of sticks! So he wouldn't have wanted to be reminded of his old name in any case. To us he was always just 'Donk' and he taught us nearly all we know about donkeys - and about a lot of other things as well.

The first thing he insisted was, that donkeys need to be one of the family. He loved coming into the kitchen and would spend dreamy hours just standing there, in the middle of all the dogs, being 'one of us'. He loved coming in at meal times best and his softly-snuffling nose would investigate all our curious food with great interest.

His manners were always perfect. He even taught behaviour to some of the dogs. When a new one barked at him, he just looked down on it tolerantly and blew a warm donkey-breath to calm it down.

His back was weak, so he found giving rides difficult. However he solved the problem in his own tactful way. He didn't buck or kick the would-be rider. He just stood stock still and nothing in Heaven or on earth would budge him.

"Sit on me and welcome," he would say, "But that is all I can manage."

He came to us with a twisted foot. But under Ben Steven the farrier's skilful care it became better and better until eventually it was quite cured.... until you bent down and whispered quietly,

"How is your poor foot today, Donk?"

And then he would raise it with tender concern and begin to limp ever so realistically... until he forgot and walked normally again!

Our years with Donk were so quiet and uneventful that we lost count of them all too quickly. He was part of our lives and, like children, we took it for granted he would last for ever.

He loved the hot summer days but the cold and the wet of each successive winter took their toll. Finally, when he had shepherded us carefully through his last Christmas, he ambled away as peacefully and as uncomplainingly as ever and took with him a little corner of all our hearts.

We buried him in his field, in the shade of the big apple-tree. The tits nest in the trunk above his head and the grass grows sweet and green all around...

CHAPTER XII

SADDLED WITH A HORSE

We have been owned by three donkeys so far and have played host to quite a few others who have agreed to tolerate our hospitality as a 'lay-by' in their wanderings through life.

Once they had become used to being donkey pastures, the two paddocks seemed to enjoy it almost as much as we did. But I don't think they actually intended us to branch out any further than that..

"'Three-quarters of an acre of fine Sussex grazing," they agreed together, smugly, "That should be enough for any self-respecting household however animal-bewitched they are.." and for once, I was inclined to agree with them.

Typical of life, I must say, that once having so satisfactorily solved the problem of keeping down the rampant growth on one acre that not all that long afterwards we found ourselves paying for the extra rental of the adjoining two acres of grassland. Sometimes we could have even done with more again!

How come, I'd like to know, that the two most unhorse-minded parents this side of Newmarket succeeded in breeding a pony-besotted daughter like Jenny grew up to be?

I could say, "Pony-mad" but it doesn't describe it nearly accurately enough. When I think of Jenny and her pony and how they grew closer and closer together with every year that passed, I can believe, more than ever, in some form of animal magic!

Sometimes I swear you could have popped a pony head on Jenny's young shoulders and she would have no more noticed the difference than did Puck's Bottom the Weaver.

I am talking big, of course, because I am frightened. It is horses, they always scare me. They don't frighten me because I think they are going to hurt me. Bless them, most of them have better manners than many humans... or dogs! But because they, themselves, are so terribly vulnerable.

Their very size makes them vulnerable. Those long legs! One break and the poor horse is gone for ever and oh, the heartbreak that remains!

And the way they are bartered around from one owner to another, like slaves, to be bought and sold at the whim of a spoilt Junior... and often so very, very, alone!

I look at it completely the wrong way round I know, according to the Pony world. So, I am glad to say, did both of our first, two offspring.

Katherine now, all she asked for was to move into the country and to have a dog. Soon after we arrived in Sussex, she found that the two-legged variety of local life was even more interesting than the four... and, thank God, they don't eat grass!

Elizabeth is like me. She likes her livestock sharing her hearth and home. She goes even further than me, she likes them sharing her bed as well! It always gave me quite a turn to find her head on the first pillow and Jemima's head on the next when I called her each morning!

She certainly aided and abetted the donkey adopting enthusiastically enough, even mucked out the stable daily for the first month or two.. but there the matter rested comfortably.

We did not appreciate our luck!

We were sitting back, resting on our undeserved laurels, a snug home in the country, twelve dogs in our very successful kitchen kennels, two cats (in the airing-cupboard) and a donkey or two in the paddock, not to mention three nice daughters who had so far safely by-passed smoking, drug dens, atheism and, indeed it seemed, all the perils of adolescent life. We never even thought of a Pony-peril.

The hopeful whisper of small Jenny bounced off our over-confidence almost unnoticed.

"A pony? Heavens no! They must cost the earth!"

"Well, I'll start saving anyway."

That sounded a pretty safe occupation. You couldn't get too wealthy on the equivalent of fifteen pence a week. I felt so safe, I could even afford to be generous.

"I tell you what, how about having a ride down at the Hope in the Valley stables when there is a pound over from the dogs one Saturday?

"How right those sensible articles on 'Don't buy a pony for your daughter, Mrs. Worthington,' were. A few shillings invested in hiring someone else's were worth their weight in gold.

"Mmm, that would be super... I shall need a riding-hat, of course..." Yes well, even a hat was reasonable to a winner like this artful Mum.

... "and some boots... and some 'jods' too, look I've gone through these jeans again!"

At least there was one advantage in it all. When birthdays or Christmas came round you didn't have to put any deep thought into present choosing. The catalogue of riding accessories is a good, thick book and the wear and tear on its ingredients is unbelievably rapid.

We were coaxed nearer and nearer the touch-line.

"Of course, if I had a pony of my own now, you wouldn't have to pay for any riding lessons at all. It would be free every day and all day." Jenny's superlatives were almost as convincing as Elizabeth's had been in their time.

"I expect Donk would love to have a pony for

company, wouldn't he? It would not cost any more than he does either, just eating grass the same. Why! I should think we would save money when we have a pony!"

Yes well, We all live and learn. Well we live, anyway. What I eventually learned was that I had been ever so carefully and ever so patiently, put onto a remorselessly downward sliding path by this astonishingly determined smallest daughter of mine. And I never regained my balance or my senses until I was triumphantly landed onto the hard mud of a dealer's garden shed and slap in front of the hugest, shiniest hunk of pony imaginable!

Then I Woke up!

But far, far too late. For better or for worse, we were saddled with a horse.

Even then I tried, in vain, to cling to the optimistic dream that the worst was over. The huge bill for horse and tack was paid and now all we had to do was to sit back and admire that awfully handsome pony in our field. And he was decorative, you had to admit. He shone like a new chestnut in the sunlight and Donk adored him.

Come to think of it, for donkey owners of several years' standing, we were singularly thick in horse-economics. But you see, we had lived off the land where the donkeys were concerned. The bedding we brought home in carloads from the Common, sacks and sacks of dry fern, and not a penny to be paid for it. In fact the Preservation Society were glad to have it cut and removed! And the hay was gathered from every orchard and churchyard within easy driving radius. It was hard work but, again, it was free and the owners were glad to have it cleared away.

But with the pony we had obviously moved from the bed and board business into the select hotel service. The pony demanded straw, and only wheat straw at that. And when the first winter came, he gobbled up our proud pile of local hay before I had even started the Christmas Shopping Lists.

Then there were the horse-shoes! Goodness, it is a good thing I don't need shoes as often as a pony does. Mind you, like household plumbing and car engines, I still suspect the whole business of shoeing needs a bit of modernising, on the quiet. After all, dogs have managed to persuade their paws to stand up to hard pavements, so when are horses going to catch on?

But there, I expect I am a very biased, very ungrateful pony-Mum.

When we had made the fatal transaction with Mr. Stuckles, who is the nicest horse-dealer I have ever met, he said reassuringly to me,

"Now Mrs. Fleming, don't you worry. That pony has got a wise head on its shoulders and he is young yet. Your daughter and he will grow up together and they will teach each other as they go along."

So we took our noble Centaur homeward-bound and, after careful thought, we christened him Merlin since he was to be so wise! And really he was the absolutest, nicest pony in the world, with an endless fund of good-humour and common-sense.

Mr. Stuckles was right too, he taught young Jenny a whole curriculum of lessons. Mind you, they were not quite the lessons that immediately spring to mind in the upbringing of your budding daughter. No help with arithmetic, except in calculating sacks of pony-nuts or bales of hay. No help in biology except in requiring gallons of 'Extra-Tail', cans of cod-liver oil and man-size jars of Vaseline...

But in his own line of business he was well up to B.Ed. standards. He taught her how to clean his

saddlery until it shone like his own, gorgeous coat. He taught her not to let the reins trail or he would promptly break them. He taught her how to clean out all the pails thoroughly or watch him die of starvation and thirst.

Merlin the Magnificent

He also taught her patience.. with horses, to get up early for horses, and to spend all her pocket money.. on horses, and her time too.. on horses. Yes, he has made a marvellous job of the teaching but it is a pity his range was so limited.

Occasionally they both really 'went to town' and spruced up every hair and whisker. Boots were shined. Clean jodhpurs and jacket emerged from hibernation, Hooves were oiled and you saw a vision of perfect horsemanship before your eyes. You couldn't help feeling chuffed, though you knew full well it certainly wasn't in your honour.

It was Gymkhana Day and all six feet were 'straining at the pedals' to be gone to join the fray. .

Goodness knows where the urge comes from. It must have been another of those secret lessons young Merlin had brain- washed our Innocent into. Actually I don't believe he liked the racing side of it nearly as much as it was claimed.

I have a strong suspicion Merlin went to the Gymkhanas because he just adored having lots and lots of other horses around.

I can see his point too. The horses were fun, all shapes and sizes, all breeds and all colours. It is their riders I was not so keen on... Talk about 'Riding your high horse!' But there, I can't even keep my balance on a high horse.

The nicest part of the day for me, was when Merlin would decide to try out one of the open horse-boxes, especially if it was the one being used for the Show Secretary's office.

He would trot up the ramp with a charming air of,

"So this is where I sign in, is it? Fine. How thoughtful of you to put the ramp down for me."

Clonk, clonk he would go to the top of the wooden slope. Then he would look engagingly around and remark,

"Ah, now, where do I put my mark?"

It always brought the house down! It nearly brought the horse-box down too! Conversely, the lowest part of the Show for me was the Jumping Ring, simply because I refuse to believe most of the horses really enjoyed jumping. I have only met one horse who actually enjoyed it. and he, unfortunately, did it so much that he jumped his way out of a great many fields too many! It can be inconvenient, so maybe it is a good thing most of them are not Kangaroos at heart.

Merlin did not mind jumping when he was in the mood. But, even when grazing in a field chock full of gates, tiger-traps, fences, and hurdles, I never saw him tryout even one quiet leap-frog on his own. So you can hardly rate it his life's ambition.

When Donk died he had a new companion in the field, and we had the prettiest little Jenny donkey in the world.

They made a marvellous pair together. He treated her very like a younger sister, liked to have her around, shared the hay with her and stood guard while she curled up in the stable at night.

Like any big brother too, he liked to think he could nuzzle her into line when she got too uppish.

She, for her part, knew that he was the ONLY pony worth having... another successful bit of brain-washing? She grazed with one ear always alert to detect any change in direction on his part and followed him, faithfully, like a little dog, wherever he led, Not that she was above cheeking him when she was in the mood or upping her dainty, hind hooves at him when the wind was in her tail. It wouldn't have

Gymkhana Day

been so much fun if she hadn't. The only rival to his affections was her best friend Victoria, who lived down the road. It was within honking distance, so they 'got on the telephone' to each other when they were feeling especially chatty. But their calls, although not long, were good and loud and, you must admit, there is nothing that quite beats a couple of chatty donkeys!

To return to the hero of our chapter.

Not for him the slave-market of the horse-exchange. No, he was firmly an institution, part of the furniture? No, part of the family. He lived to a ripe, old age, smashing to the end and king of all he surveyed. And when he passed at last to the green pastures of the Great Beyond he took with him an epitaph any horse would be proud to acknowledge, from his sorrowing owner: - "I have lost my best friend."

Good Companions

CHAPTER XIII

CASTLES, COTTAGES
AND KINDNESS

It is over forty years now since we sprang the trap of suburbia and headed south, out of the rat-race, for ever. Like Noah we have steered our cargo of livestock over many waters before we have reached our present haven in the shape of a tiny cottage in a hamlet with the glorious name of Golden Cross in the heart of the incredibly beautiful countryside of Sussex.

I've been counting up. Our freight, through the years, has numbered sixty-eight dogs, forty-one cats, five donkeys, three ponies, twelve rabbits, four guinea-pigs, gold-fish, tortoises.. .and the mice that I have stopped counting because I do get lost when there are too many noughts. Oh and one bat!

Hamsey Church

The bat was our easiest guest by far. I found him, frozen, on the floor of the old Hamsey Church that we cleaned every week. He sat on the front seat of my car for the journey home, to thaw him out, as though he had been chauffeur-driven all his life, and quite unconcerned by a very confused Labrador snuffling and drooling over him from the back seat. He enjoyed the view from the empty cat-run I put him into to recover and then he said, "No, thank you, you've been very kind (and warming) but I won't stay the night. I must be off back to my belfry. I'll just squeeze through your netting - I'm not much more than a mouse after all.." And with that, away he flew.

Actually the loft here is full of bats! But we go our ways in distant courtesy, except of course for the baby who fell down the kitchen chimney last Summer and spent the rest of the night clinging patiently to the sitting room curtain!

So, did it work? Was it worth it, our Great Escape?

Perhaps it is a bit dangerous for me to say, "Yes, yes, yes." It might inspire the entire population of South London to up-sticks and head for Sussex until we should be so crowded here we should all have to move north again!

But that is how it is: - Yes, yes, yes.

We are on generation number three now, with six grandchildren to show for it who spread from here to the centre of North America. No, none of us have managed to accumulate more money than we need. The streets of Sussex were not paved with gold. Or more possessions than we need for everyday use. What do we have? We have friendship. We have the joy of never passing anyone along the road without giving and receiving a smile and a word of friendly greeting, even if they are complete strangers. We have the joy of looking across the fields under what Katherine so perceptively calls 'a wide sky'. There is a freedom to look far, to go in peace, and to think in depth - and to hear a thousand country sounds. We may not board many four-footed guests these days, but there are a sizeable number of visitors who need no invitation. They make their own beds and find their own food and are so welcome it is our privilege to have them.

The house-martins and swallows, for instance, who swoop in to land after that incredible journey half-way across the World. "We're home, we're home," they sing and disappear under the eaves and into the stable, twittering and singing to their hearts content.

Then there are the pheasants. It is like having peacocks on the terrace in the true manorial tradition. They are so beautiful, shimmering in a rainbow of colour along the lane. You hear them clack-clacking at dawn and at sunset and wonder at such regal, glorious birds making such a hideously raucous noise. Still, it's the same with all the larger birds, the splendid jays, the impeccably designed magpies, the orientally splendid woodpecker. Not a note of music between them all!

The Woodpecker

Clearly the maker of Birds, when all the World was young, must have plunged His hands over-joyously into the barrel marked, 'Colour-birds' and showered the contents on all the big birds standing first in the queue, When it came to the turn of the little birds only the quiet browns and blacks were left. But, luckily, there was still the Song-barrel waiting there and all the little birds drank deeply of its bubbling, singing waters to make up.

So if you visit here in May you can hear the nightingale filling the countryside with his torrent of song. He is particular about his acoustics. A still, warm night is the best, when he floods the silence with trill after trill, now one song, now another, singing out his happiness to you and to the stars.

When the snow lies thick on the ground, the moorhens, from the farmpond next-door, hurry up the paddock to join in the hunt for tit-bits under the nut-holders. The blackbirds start up at first light calling, "Where's our breakfast? Where's our breakfast." And the robin sings his heart out in the willow tree to thank us for spreading the bird-table with his favourite food.

Down every winding lane there is a castle

Yes, children and grand-children alike, the life we found in this Sussex heart-land has marked us all for life. Come to think of it, they are all creditable sprigs of the original Mr. and Mrs. Noah of Old Testament times. Katherine and Doug now have seven much-loved cats indoors and a varying number of semi-wild ones out of doors. Elizabeth lives in a house which looks, to my Anglo-Saxon eyes, a small offspring of the White House itself (though she swears it is all wood and plastic really). That not withstanding, it is home to: - one dog, three cats, one rabbit, one guinea-pig, and an African hedgehog, all of which have the run of all three floors, plus hamsters, fish-tanks and a rapidly-growing Australian frog. Outside in the garden there are squirrels and chipmunks and a rainbow of coloured birds (all with an American accent I guess!) and inside, at night, Elizabeth and her tolerant husband, Steve, still share board and bed (literally) with any of their household who care to join them!

Jenny and her husband Dave's cottage has a paddock beside it for the dear old rescue pony who amicably shares his stable with the swallows and his field with the rabbits, moles and passing foxes. Their Golden Retriever is a gallant successor to Toffee, and my dog, successor to my beloved Lucy, is, believe it or not, an irrepressible Yorkshire Terrier with a heart as large as her body is small.

Yes, we have all found our individual Mt. Ararat, each in our own way. For me there was a wonderful extra bonus. Well, lots of bonuses actually. How many more can I have? A life full of so many happinesses, and even the chance to write about them! And, at a much deeper level, the chance to live and, more over, to be accepted, in a part of England that, for me, enshrines the heart of her long and glorious history. In Sussex here the Romans marched and disappeared, Saxon and

Norman clashed in battle. By Lewes town our freedom was regained in further fight. Here the Martyrs burned for even deeper freedom and here was the front-line of a nation called to arms in 1939 to face a deadly foe and save the Western World!

The streets of Sussex may not be paved with gold but they are rich to overflowing in history. Here, down every winding lane is a castle, or an ancient manor-house, a flint-cased church or a barn that has sheltered food and flocks for years too many to number while every little town and village keeps hidden a treasure-chest of relics and, with them, a secret pride in a history that spans a thousand years or more.

When I shop in Lewes I walk the path where those first Saxons trod, or I climb (breathless, these days!) the hill where Prince Edwards' knights rode confidently to their downfall six hundred years ago. In Alfriston the nights still ring ghostly with the muffled trotting of the smugglers' ponies, and down at Pevensey Bay, the tide still swirls over the stony strand where Romans and then Normans first beached their threatening boats.

To let memory come full circle, back to that momentous day when I first knocked on the 'door of our dreams' under the sardonic glance of one towering Scots pine. Even then there was history still in the making. For, On the night of October the fifteenth 1987 and into the early hours of the sixteenth, the Hurricane swept up the English Channel and bulldozed its way across this corner of South-east England. .

It thudded, like a battering ram against the old house which still stood firm. But the pine-tree, its old arms spread wide in blessing as they had stood for a hundred years, fought manfully back, hour after hour, until it could fight no more. Suddenly it began to keel slowly down from the storm-ridden sky.

Down and down it came, brushing one of the huge Victorian chimneys carelessly through the roof as it passed, until at last it hit the lawn, bounced once, and then lay still. The topmost branches tangled with the last of the honeysuckle twined around the gate-posts sixty feet from where its roots heaved out of the heavy clay that had been its nursery and its home for all of its life.

A hundred years of history fell with it. When it had been just high enough, it had stared into the study window to watch the children in their button-boots and knickerbockers playing with their wooden dolls... The pony and trap had stood elegantly in the drive way, and the big cart horse had patiently ploughed the field across the railway line. The old Queen still reigned as matriarch of all Europe and two big tom-cats sat complacently in front of the black kitchen range. .

As he grew, so the trains hurtled at his feet faster and noisier. The little trap became a snorting automobile overnight, the field was laid out as a garden and tennis-court and ladies in sweeping dresses wielded their raquets with a delicate grace.

Then wars and rumours of wars. The throb of bombers overhead, the wail of sirens through the night. And then -US!

Well, at least, in his twilight years old 'pine-tree never lacked for company, or variety, or, in a strange way, love. Old Victorian at heart as he always was, he stood for all the finest qualities of a dying age. For uprightness and truth, for courage against the storms and batterings of life, for loyalty and steadfastness, and - if you looked up to see 'him outlined clear against the wide, blue sky - for hope.'

He had watched us as we had slowly metamorphosed from clumsy townies into almost respectable country-dwellers. Somehow he had become a symbol of our success. I remember how, if you were right away up on the top of the Downs that lined our southern sky, you could always mark out our house and home by the old pine tree standing like a black spire out of the flat Wealden landscape.... A pine tree on Mount Ararat!

We have a pine-tree here. Only a baby really, hardly twenty feet high. But the nightingale sometimes chooses him to sing from on early summer nights away down the paddock. So life goes on, but how different our own lives would have been if we had not followed our star and made our Great Escape!

Do you know what the latest name for it is, in the hideously ugly vernacular of this so prosaic decade? 'Down-shifting'! It doesn't describe it properly, does it? 'Up-shifting' might be better, more uplifting, more hopeful.. And hope and faith is what is needed to change the whole direction of one's life, and that of one's family as well, from the hurtling speed of the

Main Line onto the peaceful, untrendy, wandering of the Local Line. Down here we call it the 'Bluebell Line', and that, I may say, in conclusion, sums it up to perfection!

And when the line turns itself into a country track it leads you through meadow and woodland, through birdsong and blackberries, and becomes the 'Cuckoo Trail.'

Follow that and you will find this real England that you had thought was lost and gone for ever! This country of castles, cottages and kindness. 'This green and pleasant land', 'this earth, this realm this England'!

The Family

A TAIL TO END MY TAIL

When God had made the earth and sky
The flowers and the trees
He then made all the animals
And all the birds and bees.
And when His work was finished
Not one was quite the same.
He said, "I'll walk this earth of mine
And give each one a name."
And so He travelled land and sea
And everywhere He went
A little creature followed Him
Until its strength was spent.
When all were named upon the earth
And in the sky and sea,
The little creature said, "Dear Lord,
There's not one left for me."
The Father smiled and softly said:
"I've left you to the end.
I've turned my own name back to front
And called you Dog, my friend."

(Anon)